Praise for

5 STEPS TO EXPERT

"If you are serious about yourself and your life's work, this is the perfect guidebook! You hold in your hands the blueprint for how to achieve success—applicable in the classroom, the boardroom, or the locker room. Leave it to an expert to document what it takes to join him in the top 5 percent!"

—Bob Rathbun, Emmy award–winning play-by-play broadcaster for Fox Sports Net and professional speaker

"Finally! A book that gives us the real formula to achieve success and enhance our expertise, and delivers that formula with the impact of a bullet train—hard driving, efficient, and on track. Now there are no more excuses for not being the person others look to as a model for success. The exercises in this book force you to be brutally honest with yourself and pinpoint exactly what you need to achieve your goals. If you want to become the expert others envy and emulate, this book is for you."

—Diane Bogino, Performance Strategies, Inc.; author, *Finding Your Bootstraps* and *There's Something Funny About Humor in Presentations*

"5 Steps to Expert *offers busy executives some food for thought and practical advice about how to develop capacity and expertise for the demands of modern business, and how to find an extra gear of mental performance. This book provides a nice framework for addressing a lot of the issues we are currently facing in executive education.*"

— **Dr. Kevin Morris, Director of Executive Development, University of Auckland Business School, New Zealand**

5 STEPS TO EXPERT

5

STEPS TO EXPERT

How to Go from Business Novice to Elite Performer

PAUL G. SCHEMPP

Davies-Black Publishing
Mountain View, California

Published by Davies-Black Publishing, a division of CPP, Inc., 1055 Joaquin Road, 2nd Floor, Mountain View, CA 94043; 800-624-1765.

Special discounts on bulk quantities of Davies-Black books are available to corporations, professional associations, and other organizations. For details, contact the Director of Marketing and Sales at Davies-Black Publishing: 650-691-9123; fax 650-623-9271.

Visit the Davies-Black Publishing Web site at www.daviesblack.com.

Printed in the United States of America.
12 11 10 09 08 10 9 8 7 6 5 4 3 2 1

Library of Congress Cataloging-in-Publication Data
    Schempp, Paul G.
    5 steps to expert : how to go from business novice to elite performer / Paul G.
    Schempp
       p. cm.
    Includes bibliographical references and index.
    ISBN: 978-0-89106-114-4 (hardcover)
    1. Vocational qualifications. 2. Performance. 3. Expertise. 4. Career development.
    I. Title. II. Title: Five steps to expert
    HF381.6.S34 2008
    650.1—dc22

2008015768

FIRST EDITION
First printing 2008

CONTENTS

List of Expertise Exercises ix
About the Author xi
Preface xiii

INTRODUCTION
The Journey Toward Becoming Expert 1

ONE
The Three Keys to Expertise 11

TWO
Beginning as a Beginner 27

THREE
Converting to Capable 43

FOUR
Cultivating Competence 59

FIVE
Practicing Proficiency 79

SIX
Excelling to Expert 99

SEVEN
Navigating the Journey 127

Afterword 145
Notes 147
References 155
Index 161

EXPERTISE EXERCISES

1. Rating Your Expertise 8

2. Expertise Key 1: Your Experience 24

3. Expertise Key 2: Your Knowledge 25

4. Expertise Key 3: Your Skills 25

5. Identifying Rules to Live By 40

6. Learning from Experience 41

7. Meeting Mentors 42

8. Responding to Situations 57

9. Developing Strategic Knowledge 57

10. Maximizing Resources 58

11. Guiding Actions with Goals and Long-Term Plans 75

12. Distinguishing What's Important in Your Business World 76

13. Planning Your Options 77

14. Developing Your Critical Skills 78

15. Taking Responsibility 95

16. Performing Routine Tasks 95

17. Making Decisions That Make a Difference 96

18. Harnessing Outside Resources 97

19. Self-Monitoring 124

20. Networking 125

21. Devising an Expert Action Plan 126

ABOUT THE AUTHOR

Paul G. Schempp, PhD, named the 2004 Distinguished Scholar by the International Center for Performance Excellence at West Virginia University, has dedicated his professional life to understanding what it takes to be an expert performer. As a professor at the University of Georgia, he has spent more than a decade conducting award-winning research into the characteristics and development of expertise. His research has made him a much-sought-after keynote speaker for professional meetings and corporate conferences, including the American Society for Training and Development, BASF Corp., the Buckhead Business Association, the Club Corporation of America, the National Association for Sport and Physical Activity, the National Institute of Education (Singapore), the Swedish Golf Federation, the Society for Human Resource Management, and the Swiss Soccer Federation.

Schempp, president of Performance Matters, Inc., has more than twenty-five years of experience in the fields of research, education, and professional development. The author of four books, he is an internationally renowned speaker, scholar, and consultant. He has served as a Senior Fulbright Research Scholar at the University of Frankfurt (Germany) and as a visiting professor at the Nanyang Technical University (Singapore).

PREFACE

They make it look so easy. Whether it's Alex Rodriguez playing baseball, Maya Angelou reciting poetry, Donald Trump closing a deal, Warren Buffett investing in a promising venture, or Bono on stage, their actions appear elegant and effortless. So natural are experts that it seems impossible that they ever struggled to achieve their signature greatness. These elite performers seem to exude a talent few others are privileged to possess. Or, so I thought.

Like most people, I always wanted to be good at what I did. The truth? I wasn't. But the realization that I wasn't very good at most things I tried never deterred me from the belief that I could be. I watched others who were good and thought, *I* could do that. But how? What was it they were doing that I was not? Therein began my journey to discover what it takes to be an expert.

For the record, I'm still on that journey and still far from completing it. There has been some progress, however. In fact, one writer has described me as an "expert on expertise."[1] While such remarks are flattering, much remains to be explored and discovered despite nearly twenty years of studying experts and helping professional athletes and business professionals develop their expertise.

As a professor at a major research university, my investigation into expertise allows me the privilege of studying many successful and interesting people. By sharing with others what I've learned about becoming expert, I have been richly rewarded. Experts in many diverse fields have shown their kindness by describing to me what has helped them on their journey. The feedback I've received from speaking to professional, business, and sports organizations around the world has convinced me that many people are not only seeking to become more expert in what they do but also succeeding in their quest for excellence. From organizations such as the American Society for Training and Development, corporations such as BASF, and professional athletes such as European PGA star Niclas Fasth, I have discovered that understanding the steps to expert helps people become better at what they do. This book was written to help you on your journey. It is a journey we obviously share, or you wouldn't be reading these words. Let's get started.

I thought I'd be a great teacher. I had no doubt. I loved children, loved my subject, and—bottom line—it didn't look all that hard. I had a wake-up call, however, during my senior year in college while I was student teaching. I felt fortunate to be placed with John Hichwa at John Read Middle School in Redding, Connecticut. Almost immediately I realized that there was magic to his teaching. John had a way of touching lives as he taught children. I couldn't put my finger on it because he made teaching look easy, natural—as if it required no effort at all. John got extraordinary results, while my attempts resulted in a collection of confused looks on my students' faces and chaos in the classroom. Clearly, I was not ready to teach, so I decided to pursue graduate school to better study teachers and how they achieved great things. There, I learned to be a researcher. I studied great teachers and then great coaches. Now I study experts of any kind.

By studying experts, I have discovered that becoming expert is not innate behavior. The more experts I interview in more and more fields, this becomes increasingly clear: Experts are not born; they are self-made—they earn it. They earn it by gaining experience, by acquiring knowledge, and by developing skills. Jeff Thull makes this point clearly in his book *Exceptional Selling* when he writes about expert sales professionals: "Contrary to the popular image of salespeople as 'born communicators,' most people, and that includes salespeople, are not naturally effective communicators."[2]

Experts develop in specific, predictable steps—five to be exact. No matter how great people become in their field, they all start as a beginner. Alex Rodriguez, Maya Angelou, Donald Trump, Warren Buffett, and Bono were all beginners at one time.

Because of my work on experts and the development of expertise, I was invited to serve as a performance consultant for the Swedish Golf Federation. I was challenged to discover through theory and research which expertise skills, if any, would produce results in a sport. Swedish golf is a bit of an unexpected phenomenon. Sweden is known more for snow and ice than lush, green golf courses. You would expect to find outstanding skiers and hockey players in Sweden, not golfers. But, with innovative coaches, open-minded athletes, and the support of a dedicated federation, much is possible. The record of success gained by Swedish golfers, both men and women, is rivaled by very few countries. By way of example, in the 2002 Open Golf Championship in Muirfield, Scotland, only the United States, with a significantly larger population and more conducive golf climate, had more players in the field than Sweden. And while it would be overly simplistic and a mistake to think that the principles of expertise development alone accounted for this success, success followed when these principles were applied.

Sports is not the only domain that has sought out and applied the principles of developing expertise—that is, moving people along the journey from beginner to expert. Corporations and professional associations are increasing their search for additional information about how their leaders, employees, and members can become consistently outstanding performers. The point is this: If you are willing to learn what it takes to become expert and are willing to apply these principles in practice, you will elevate your level of expertise and success.

While experts represent only a small percentage of the top performers in a field, everyone can become *more* expert in what they do. And that brings us to this book, which was written to share what I and other researchers have discovered about becoming expert. In this book, you can read about the research and hear the stories of those who have committed themselves to the journey toward becoming expert. By knowing the keys and steps to developing expertise, you too can become more expert in your trade, business, or profession.

THE JOURNEY TOWARD BECOMING EXPERT

Mr. Scheidler was a history teacher at Martinsville High School in Indiana. Like many good teachers, he often discussed topics ranging beyond his subject area in an effort to guide his students in directions that would help them lead happy, productive, and successful lives. One March afternoon, Mr. Scheidler challenged his class to write a paper defining success. He wanted to start those young minds thinking about the concept of success and whether it means just becoming rich or famous or just winning a ball game. A sophomore thought hard about the topic. He continued thinking about the topic for a long time after completing Mr. Scheidler's homework assignment. In fact, he reflected on that assignment for decades.

In struggling to find an answer to the question Mr. Scheidler posed, the student also recalled the advice his father had frequently given him when he was growing up on the family farm: Don't worry much about trying to be better than someone else. Sometime later, the young man wrote this about his father's lessons: "Dad always added the following. 'Always try to be the very best that *you* can be.

Learn from others, yes. But don't just try to be better than they are. You have no control over that. Instead try, and try very hard, to be the best that you can be. That you have control over. Maybe you'll be better than someone else and maybe you won't. That part of it will take care of itself.'"[1]

Years later, that young man became a high school teacher himself, and he also began coaching. The lessons learned through Mr. Scheidler's assignment and his father's teachings followed him and became principles he lived by. In 1934, while teaching English and coaching basketball at Central High School in South Bend, Indiana, John Wooden put to paper the single sentence he had reflected on for so long: "Success is a peace of mind, which is a direct result of self-satisfaction in knowing you made the effort to become the best you are capable of becoming."[2] Leaving behind the classroom, Coach Wooden pursued a career as a college basketball coach and went on to lead UCLA to ten NCAA championships, seven in a row—a feat that has never been equaled and many believe never will be.

John Wooden was not born an expert basketball coach. He *learned* to be successful—in sports and in life. The search for ways by which people's endeavors can be promoted and improved has produced a fertile body of knowledge. Despite a long, rich, and rewarding journey, the search is far from over. The hunt for excellence in human performance has led to the exploration of many new areas. The development of expertise is among them. We long to know what it takes to be the best.

Scholars and scientists have attempted to unravel the mysteries and complexities surrounding the development and actions of those sitting atop the pinnacle of human performance. Though only a few scholars are currently investigating the phenomenon of extraordinary performance, their work has been vigorous and varied. Today, we know a great deal more about becoming expert than we did just twenty years ago. Because this knowledge has been collected from experts in fields ranging from waiters and taxi drivers to nurses, surgeons, and military generals, this body of knowledge offers a rich resource for virtually anyone undertaking nearly any endeavor.

Tracing the development of experts from a variety of fields has made it possible to identify the steps experts follow in climbing to the top. At each step, or level, of expertise, the common characteristics that indicate that level have also been identified—regardless of the business, profession, or trade—or any other human endeavor. Stanford Graduate School of Business professor Charles O'Reilly makes the point that there is little difference between achieving success in business or in sports. For example, in the initial rounds of a golf or tennis tournament, players of differing abilities all begin at the same place. But, as the tournament progresses, the weaker performers are inevitably eliminated and the stronger performers advance.

> If you think about performance in organizations as being a function of motivation times ability—how smart you are and how hard you work—what makes a difference at the top level is effort; ability has been equilibrated. If somebody does 500 backhands a day and somebody else does only 100, then in the long-term, the person who does the more backhands is more likely to win. In one of our studies, we found that effort and ability by themselves don't appear to explain much, but the combination really matters. In other words, people who work harder, who are smarter, are going to have greater success.[3]

While the principles of expertise development are applicable to most aspects of life, they apply best to performance-oriented activities. After all, experts are those who consistently outperform their peers. In contemporary culture, few fields demand greater results from the performance of their personnel than business and industry. With issues of succession planning, workforce retention and development, and the continual pressure to achieve more with fewer resources facing every aspect of business today, developing the expertise of industry leaders, executives, and employees has never been more critical.

The Road Map

This book provides a road map for anyone in business—new graduates, staff, first-time or experienced managers, leaders, or executives—who aspire to advance from their present level of competence to higher levels of skill, knowledge, and performance. Specific characteristics that distinguish each of the five levels of expertise are described. With this information, you can identify your (or others') present expertise level—an important prerequisite to understanding how you arrived where you are and what next steps toward outstanding performance you need to take.

This book, however, provides more than just understanding of those steps. It suggests effective ways of learning based on your present level of expertise and offers a series of progressive tasks and activities to guide you through each step toward becoming expert. Each chapter includes a description of the learning modalities and strategies that can most effectively move you to the next level of expertise. Case studies, stories, and practical examples illustrate how the characteristics within each step can move you forward in your quest to become more expert in your chosen field. Developmental exercises at the end of each chapter provide checklists and worksheets to help you plan effective strategies to increase your experience, knowledge, and skills—the three keys to expertise—to improve your professional performance. These developmental exercises will help you transition smoothly to the next level.

Chapter 1 opens with the three keys to expertise. The level of expertise you ultimately achieve is primarily dependent not on any characteristic, trait, or quality you were born with or anything you may have been given, but rather on these three keys. Each key is under your control and instrumental in moving through the five steps to expert:

1. Beginner
2. Capable
3. Competent
4. Proficient
5. Expert

Each step, as described separately in chapters 2–6, includes a learning strategy to move you to the next step. Research that supports each step and behavioral attribute, particularly as it applies to business and the workplace, is included. Each chapter contains real-world business or sports examples of that step's behavioral characteristics and learning modalities. Chapter 7 offers suggestions that have proven useful in navigating the journey from business novice to elite performer.

Climbing the Steps

You cannot go directly from step 1 to step 5—from beginner to expert. As your experience, knowledge, and skills increase, you move from one step to the next, developing new characteristics that will help you perform at the next step.

The earliest, and most often cited, work on the stages of expertise development was *What Computers Can't Do* by Hubert Dreyfus in 1972.[4] His model proposed five stages to becoming expert: (1) novice, (2) advanced beginner, (3) competent, (4) proficient, and (5) expert. Since that time, a steady stream of research has revealed a great deal more information about the steps required for becoming an expert.

The steps to becoming expert represent a developmental process. When people are identified as competent, it implies that the majority of characteristics they exhibit are within the competent step. They may still hold some beginner characteristics, while at the same time may have acquired a few proficient, or perhaps even expert, characteristics.

Personal development is an individual endeavor, and none of us develops in the same way, at the same time, or for the same reasons. You, however, determine where you stop in developing your expertise—if you stop at all. You can ascend the steps, remain on your present step, or even descend the steps. Being competent today does not guarantee that you will be competent tomorrow. If you do not keep abreast of important new information, keep your skill set well honed, or learn from your increasing experience, you may find yourself at a lower level of expertise as the standards of success rise ever higher.

Climbing the steps to becoming expert does not mean that some of the lower-level characteristics are no longer applicable. Experts can still learn by someone else's example just as they did when they were a beginner. Performers who are proficient still use strategic knowledge to help them make insightful decisions, just as they did when they were at the capable level of expertise. Therefore, see these steps to expert as a guide, not a prescription, for becoming more expert in what you do. Becoming expert, in short, means becoming the best you can be at what you do.

An Invitation

I am inviting you to take a journey—a journey toward becoming expert. By the time you finish reading this book, you should understand why you do so many things well and why there are some things you do not do so well. More important, you should understand how to improve just about everything you do—particularly those things that mean the most to you and have the most impact on your professional performance. The ideas shared in this book can help anyone do just about anything better. Research has proven it. People have proven it. And this book will prove it to you.

Before beginning the journey, complete expertise exercise 1 to gauge your current level. Next, read chapter 1 about the three keys to expertise to understand how to increase your performance. Then you will be ready to undertake the journey, which begins with chapter 2, "Beginning as a Beginner." Even if you are not a beginner, I encourage you to start there to better understand where you have come from. It also will help you recognize when other people are at this step and how you might help them on their journey. Of course, if you are in fact a beginner, that is the place for you to start.

RATING YOUR EXPERTISE

Choose only the response that best answers each question.

1. How many years have you been in your present position?
   - a. ____ 0–1 year
   - b. ____ 2–4 years
   - c. ____ 5–9 years
   - d. ____ 10–14 years
   - e. ____ 15 or more years

2. Where do you learn most of the new information you use in your current position?
   - a. ____ Experience
   - b. ____ Mentor
   - c. ____ Colleagues
   - d. ____ Conferences, seminars
   - e. ____ Reading

3. Which of the following most often guides your decision making?
   - a. ____ Rules and norms
   - b. ____ The situation
   - c. ____ Long-term goals
   - d. ____ Results from a careful analysis of the problem
   - e. ____ Intuition

4. When assessing the outcomes of your professional actions, what percentage is normally due to your actions versus external or situational factors?
   - a. ____ 10 percent
   - b. ____ 25 percent
   - c. ____ 50 percent
   - d. ____ 75 percent
   - e. ____ 90 percent

5. If 10 were all the knowledge a person could possibly have to do your job and 0 were no knowledge at all, where would you rate your current level of knowledge?

    a. _____ 8

    b. _____ 7

    c. _____ 6

    d. _____ 5

    e. _____ 4

6. When planning occurs in your workplace, you

    a. _____ Are seldom involved

    b. _____ Like to see how things were done previously

    c. _____ Always have a primary plan and a backup plan

    d. _____ Gather all the pertinent information before attempting a plan

    e. _____ Usually analyze the results of your actions after plan execution

7. In the past twelve months, how many books have you read that have helped you in some way in your current position?

    a. _____ None

    b. _____ 1

    c. _____ 2–3

    d. _____ 4–5

    e. _____ 6 or more

8. When something does not go as planned or fails in your workplace, recently you have found that the reason is

    a. _____ Outside forces (e.g., competition, customers)

    b. _____ Failure to clearly communicate goals, expectations, or procedures within your organization

    c. _____ Lack of collaborative planning

    d. _____ Your team's failure to adequately anticipate or analyze the problem

    e. _____ Your decisions or actions

(cont'd)

EXPERTISE EXERCISE 1 CONT'D

9. If your on-the-job performance over the the past twelve months were measured, where would that performance rank against that of other people in your organization or in a position similar to yours?

   a. ____ 25% or below

   b. ____ Top 25–50%

   c. ____ Top 50–75%

   d. ____ Top 75–95%

   e. ____ I would be the top performer

10. In matters related to your business or profession, you find that you can remember

   a. ____ Most of what you were told is important for the job

   b. ____ Most of what is necessary to get the job done

   c. ____ Enough to do the job right

   d. ____ The most important information for making a sound decision

   e. ____ Every detail that might have an influence on the final outcome

---

SCORING YOUR EXPERTISE

Tally your responses using the following scale:

   a = 1
   b = 2
   c = 3
   d = 4
   e = 5

Total points: _____

Circle your level of expertise based on your total points:

   5–10   Beginner
   11–20   Capable
   21–35   Competent
   36–45   Proficient
   46–50   Expert

ONE

THE THREE KEYS TO EXPERTISE

If you are attracted to fad diets to lose weight, lottery tickets to gain wealth, and the latest fashion statement to make yourself attractive, put this book down. You cannot be born to expertise, nor buy it or borrow it. You have to work at it. No exceptions. And you cannot work at it for just one day, one week, one month, or even one year. You have to work at it for years—many years. But, if you love what you do, then a labor of love is a highly attractive proposition.

Experts: Made, Not Born

No one is born an expert. Some people may be fortunate to be endowed with certain physical, mental, social, or emotional characteristics that help them pursue superior performances. Those characteristics alone, however, have never made anyone an expert. In fact, what some people have overcome in the pursuit of elite achievement is often as inspirational as it is remarkable.

Bobby's Shoes

Bobby's sneakers told him that he was growing, but it wasn't that the sneakers would become tight. As Bobby tells his story,

> They bought them for me extra big. The foster mom I lived with showed me how to crinkle up tissues and push them tight into the front of the sneaker. She told me that as my feet grew, I would need less tissues and take some out. So sometimes I'd check to see if I was growing by pulling out the tissues from each sneaker, remove a few, crinkle the rest, and fill the toe back up. That's how I knew I was growing, as the sneaker space shrunk, I knew I was growing bigger. Only problem was that nothing else in my life grew. My school awards didn't grow, so I didn't think my mind grew much. My friends didn't grow, 'cause I never stayed anywhere long enough to see anyone. All I have to show are these sneakers. And I don't even like them. Whenever I look at them I think about how they are all scuffed up . . . just like me, just like I'm scuffed up. No shine on my shoes. No shine on me.[1]

When he became a young man, Bobby got a job in a fruit and vegetable store. Every week he saved a small portion of his paycheck. One day he had saved enough to make his first real purchase—a pair of shoes. But they were not just any shoes. He bought a shiny pair of cordovan-colored shoes that he polished every day. His shoes carried him to a job as an office boy at the Albany, New York, *Times Union* newspaper. As his experience, knowledge, and skills increased, he continued walking up the corporate staircase until he reached the top, where he would spend nearly two decades as CEO of the Hearst Newspaper Group and vice president of the Hearst Corporation. Was it some innate characteristic, a birthright, or an inherent talent that took Bobby Danzig from scruffy, oversized sneakers to the corner office of a corporate empire? Unlikely.

The idea that talent makes you successful is folly. Perhaps that's why more often than not we hear about the people who never reached their potential or the can't-miss kid who missed. This point was driven home to me by one of my students at Kent State University. In the summer of 1984, Thomas Jefferson, or T.J. to those who know him best, qualified for the U.S. Olympic Team. In doing so, he fulfilled his dream to compete for the country he loves in a sport he loves in an event he loves. When he returned to campus after qualifying for the Olympic Games, I shook his hand to congratulate him. He looked me in the eye and said, "I have raced many runners a lot more talented than me. But no one ever worked harder for it than me." A few weeks later, T.J. completed his race in Los Angeles and stepped on the podium to have the Olympic bronze medal placed around his neck for his efforts in the 200-meter run.

Because expertise is neither a birthright nor an innate characteristic, most people have an opportunity to gain a high level of expertise in their chosen profession or business. Legendary business consultant Peter Drucker realized this early in his career:

> I soon learned that there is no "effective personality." The effective executives I have seen differ widely in their temperaments and their abilities, in what they do and how they do it, in their personalities, their knowledge, their interests—in fact in almost everything that distinguishes human beings. All they have in common is the ability to get the right things done. . . . Effectiveness, in other words, is a habit, that is, a complex of practices. And practices can always be learned.[2]

Using the Three Keys

If you have a passion for what you do, can identify, practice, and apply the important skills of your industry, are open to learning what others can teach you, and gain applicable experience, you will become more expert at your job. An expert is someone who consistently outperforms his or her peers. Everyone today who might be considered an expert has done this, and so can you. The secrets of their consistent and superior performance are found in factors I call the three keys to expertise:

- Experience
- Knowledge
- Skills

It is instructive to learn how these keys might best be used to elevate your performance. If you acquire and then make use of extensive experience, knowledge, and skills, you will develop expertise in what you do. Others may rival your experience, knowledge, or skills, but few will consistently outperform you.

Experience: A Great Teacher

There is no substitute for experience when it comes to developing expertise. It's when you are actually performing a task that your knowledge and skills unite to determine your level of performance. Experience offers opportunities for learning. Unfortunately, all too often people ignore the lessons offered by their experience and simply repeat the same ineffective patterns of performance. Consider your handwriting. No doubt you have been writing for years. Has the quality of your handwriting improved? Despite your extensive handwriting experience, do you consider yourself a handwriting expert? If you are like most people, despite years of experience your handwriting has not improved much, and perhaps it has even worsened. To develop your expertise, you must let experience work for you.

Thoughtfully analyzing your experiences to identify what you did well and what could be improved leads to the insights that improve performance. Perhaps reflecting on their limited practical experience, beginners find real-world practice to be their most important source of information for increasing expertise. For them, verbal or written information takes second place to trial and error in acquiring knowledge and skills.

The greater the diversity of experiences in your field—as expanded by different people, situations, and purposes—the greater is the benefit offered by those experiences. Different experiences give you opportunities to apply your knowledge and skills in new and untested ways. Some companies commonly place novice executives in various positions so that, as they climb the corporate ladder, they gain firsthand experience with various aspects of the company's operations.

Experience alone neither increases expertise nor improves performance. This point was clearly made in a study comparing high- and average-performing professional software designers.[3] The designers were all assigned a design task and asked to report the strategies they used in accomplishing the task. High performers' strategies included planning and collecting more feedback as they progressed. Further, they devoted greater attention to understanding the problem and to collaborative efforts with colleagues. Average performers spent more time analyzing the task requirements and verbalizing thoughts largely irrelevant to the problem. Despite the differences in performance quality, the designers did not differ in length of experience. In other words, the differences between the two performance groups can be explained by strategic knowledge and skills—but not by experience alone. According to Anders Ericsson,

> Improvement in performance of aspiring experts does not happen automatically or casually as a function of further experience.

Improvements are caused by changes in cognitive mechanisms mediating how the brain and nervous system control performance and in the degree of adaptation of physiological systems of the body. The principal challenge to attaining expert-level performance is to induce stable specific changes that allow the performance to be incrementally improved.[4]

Deliberate, systematic, and continual change brings about the improvements leading to expert performance.

Experience is a critical, but clearly not a singular, key to developing expertise.

The Power of Knowledge

It should be obvious that experts have extensive knowledge, but the importance of this characteristic demands that it be examined thoroughly. Experts invest significantly in learning all they can about their field. Attend a conference and you will surely see experts. Because of their extensive knowledge, experts may be least likely to acquire more information at the conference, but they got where they are, in part, because they attended seminars long before they became experts. The relationships they formed and nurtured at such meetings are one reason they are now experts. They have learned that no knowledge source is too insignificant to overlook.

When experts stop learning, they soon stop being leaders in their field. Florida State University football coach Bobby Bowden clearly recognized this fact when he said, "I have been coaching fifty-one years, and I feel like I know about 60 percent of what is out there, no, maybe 50 percent. There is so much more out there. When I stop learning and adjusting, nobody will have to tell me to retire. There ain't much wiggle room at our level. When we stop adapting, we'll be losing and I'll want out."[5]

This point is as pertinent to industry as it is to sports. In discussing the surge of the Japanese to the top of the automobile market, Volkswagen's Carl Hahn said, "We have to realize their achievement, grapple with it, and change our attitudes. We have to go and learn, we Germans, we Europeans. We have been so accustomed to teaching engineering to the world that we've lost some of our receptiveness to learning."[6]

When you stop learning, you cannot lead—those who continue to learn will soon pass you by.

There are several characteristics of experts' knowledge, common strategies used in accumulating knowledge, and a few benefits in possessing a large quantity of exploitable information. First, experts' knowledge is specific to their area of expertise. When you refer to an expert's knowledge, that knowledge is largely confined to a single field of specialty. Because you are an expert in sales does not mean you are an expert in manufacturing or management. As Paul Feltovich, Michael Prietula, and Anders Ericsson describe it, our modern "conception of expertise seems to favor the specialist and specialized skills, honed over many years of extensive training and deliberate practice. The notion of the 'expert generalist' is difficult to capture within the current explanatory systems of expertise."[7] Experts are not all-knowing individuals who can speak authoritatively on any subject, but rather they possess a great deal of knowledge pertaining to a single subject, field, or domain.

Second, experts are not necessarily any more intelligent than the average person. Experts have, as you will read in later chapters, developed skills and strategies so that they can acquire, retain, and apply large quantities of information. These skills are a result of effective memory strategies and practice rather than innate intelligence.[8] You do not acquire wisdom from your innate intelligence, but rather from multiple and continual attempts to learn all you can about what you do. Studies in a variety of fields have found that even though experts gain large amounts of knowledge related to their domain, they never believe they know all there is to know about their particular area and thus continue their search for useful information.[9]

The increased experience and practice that elevates your expertise also improves your knowledge. Specifically, as you gain experience and skills, your knowledge is reorganized in ways that enable you to both retain and access information efficiently. Your knowledge becomes organized into larger, more meaningful units and thus makes it possible to remember more and use more of what you remember.[10]

The accumulated knowledge of experts provides them with more options and alternatives in planning and executing action. In a study of differences between experts and beginners, I found that more knowledgeable professionals were able to devise more alternatives in situations and construct a greater number of solutions to problems than were beginners.[11]

Experts enjoy talking almost endlessly about their subject, gathering others' views on pertinent topics, and having extensive libraries devoted to their field. They use extensive resources to build a large store of knowledge. Experience and peers have been most often identified as key sources of experts' knowledge, but books, workshops, certification programs, journals and magazines, experiences, and even clients have been identified as important knowledge sources.

One of the world's greatest entrepreneurs, Sam Walton, offers an excellent example of an expert who never stopped building his knowledge. He often talked with his frontline employees because he believed that "the ones on the front lines—the ones who talk with the customer—are the ones who really know what's going on out there. You better find out what they know."[12] Sam read extensively. As computers came into their own, Sam read all he could about them. He became so enthralled with the potential of computers that he enrolled in an IBM school and later hired some of their experts to help him expand Wal-Mart into the largest retailer in the world.

While experience and knowledge are important keys to expertise, they are not sufficient for the superior performance that is the signature of experts. Experience and knowledge provide the critical foundation for decision making, but achieving outstanding performance takes more than thinking—it takes action. And the actions of experts are defined by their skills. In other words, it is experts' highly developed skill sets that permit them to act in ways leading to consistently superior performance.

Developing Essential Skills

Children with learning disabilities are often believed to have limited chances for success, and those with severe disabilities are often dismissed as hopeless or useless before even reaching the starting line of gainful employment. Imagine leaving high school having failed mathematics repeatedly and having been stigmatized since childhood because of dyslexia. In short, by age sixteen you could neither read nor write with even a functional capacity. This was precisely the hand dealt to young Sir Richard Branson.[13] We often hear people speak of high performers as talented in some physical or intellectual way. Branson was neither. Given his disabilities, he would never be able to read adequately a simple contract or decipher the balance sheet of a corporation. What Branson could do was develop the skills that would make him successful, and as unlikely as that seems, that is precisely what he did.

While he could never become skilled at reading papers, he did become skilled at reading people, situations, and opportunities. He could never calculate the size of a profit margin, but he did learn how to calculate the depth of an individual's character. Branson used his acquired skills to found multiple corporations, including Virgin Atlantic Airways. In the process, he became a billionaire several times over. He developed the skills necessary to make him an elite business performer.

Experts' Specific Skills

The skills of an expert can be viewed as a specific set of tasks or profession-related activities that have been acquired, developed, and mastered by the expert and account for and are critical to the expert's superior performance. For example, expert chefs have superior knife-handling skills, expert salespersons have superior customer relations skills, and expert financial investors have superior strategic asset selection skills.

There is no shortage of resources for identifying skills to be practiced and perfected to have a positive effect on your performance. Often, your job description lists the key skills of your position. Mentors and colleagues can be useful in helping recognize the important skills of your business or industry. As you observe the outstanding performers in your workplace, what do you observe that accounts for their success? Finally, books such as *The 21 Irrefutable Laws of Leadership, Skills for New Managers, The Success Principles,* and *The Ultimate Competitive Advantage* have all helped people identify critical skills that propelled their performance.[14]

Experts' General Skills

Several skills are common to all experts, regardless of their field.

Each of an expert's general skills is equally important in achieving top performance.

These skills serve experts in making decisions, planning and executing actions, and evaluating performance. First, experts can distinguish the important elements from the unimportant elements in events, actions, or situations and identify which are most critical to cultivating a satisfactory response or solution. Experts can do this because they see the deeper structures of a problem—the root causes—whereas those with less expertise see only the symptoms and surface issues. Branson's ability to read people and associate with those who could make things happen is an example of the skill of identifying the important from the unimportant as it applies to people's character.

Second, experts spend more time analyzing a problem by gathering relevant information, understanding problem constraints, developing solutions, and assessing the adequacy of the attempted solutions. They like to have all the facts to devise the best strategy for moving forward. Third, experts are skilled at generating the best solutions to a given problem, and they do this faster and more accurately than nonexperts.[15]

Fourth, experts are better able to plan and implement strategies in reaching goals. They not only know which strategies are more likely to work in a given situation, but they also are more likely to use strategies with a proven track record. Fifth, experts can accurately identify deficiencies in their knowledge and skills, and locate resources or design strategies for overcoming these limitations. As good as experts are today, they strive to be better tomorrow. This might help explain how they became superior performers in the first place.

Every skill in an expert's repertoire, whether it is specific to his or her profession or general in nature, was learned. What those skills look like in action are described in chapter 6, "Excelling to Expert." How those skills are mastered is detailed in chapter 7, "Navigating the Journey."

Beginning the Journey

Every journey has a starting point, that is, a beginning. The expertise exercise you completed earlier provided an estimate of your present location along that journey. On which step are you? Beginner? Capable? Competent? Proficient? Perhaps you are already an expert. Regardless of your current level of expertise, it is helpful to understand how you got where you are and, then, where you need to go from here. Therefore, I encourage you to begin with the next chapter, "Beginning as a Beginner," which details the first steps in developing expertise, so that you know the characteristic benchmarks in becoming an expert—both for yourself and for others you may help on their journey.

Simply knowing the steps to and characteristics of becoming an expert is, however, not enough. The principles of expertise need to be purposefully practiced and applied. To achieve anything takes more than just knowing how to do something—it takes action. You decide if, when, or where the journey ends. The further you progress, the more productive you become, the better you perform, and the deeper your passion grows for what you do. The time to move forward is now. You can start by completing expertise exercises 2–4.

Summary

The three keys to expertise are

- Experience
- Knowledge
- Skills

EXPERTISE KEY 1: YOUR EXPERIENCE

Think about your professional experiences and describe a situation that provided one of your greatest learning experiences. Where did it take place? Who was involved? What happened? What did you learn?

_____

_____

_____

_____

_____

_____

_____

_____

_____

_____

_____

_____

_____

_____

_____

_____

_____

_____

_____

_____

EXPERTISE EXERCISE 3

EXPERTISE KEY 2: YOUR KNOWLEDGE

If you were designing a training program for the person who will eventually replace you, what would be the four most important training topics?

1. _____

2. _____

3. _____

4. _____

EXPERTISE EXERCISE 4

EXPERTISE KEY 3: YOUR SKILLS

Picture yourself walking alone along an empty beach and discovering an ornate glass bottle sticking out of the sand. You reach down, pull it up, and, while rubbing the sand off the bottle to better see the intricate design, you feel the bottle rumble and see smoke shooting out the top. When the smoke clears, a magnificent genie stands before you. In a deep, booming voice, he says, "I am a genie. I can make you do whatever you do better than anyone in the world. Tell me what you do." You reply: "I am a _____ [your occupation]." The genie then says, "I will make you the best at the three most important skills for a _____ [your occupation]. Just tell me what they are."

You tell him the three most important skills for your job are

1. _____

2. _____

3. _____

TWO

BEGINNING AS A BEGINNER

In any new endeavor you undertake—be it social, recreational, or occupational—you must begin as a beginner. You can't avoid it. But being a beginner is not a bad thing. To the contrary, it means you are starting on a grand adventure to attain new experiences, new knowledge, and new skills. Every journey—including the journey to expertise—begins with a single step.

Although everyone is a beginner at sometime or something, those who enter a business or profession seldom do so knowing nothing. To every new job, you bring preconceived notions of what people in that workplace do and how they do it. Your preconceptions may be based on previous experience, schooling, training, casual reading, or, perhaps, only on assumptions that may or may not be correct. You envision yourself in this job. You believe you have the requisite attitudes and qualities for the job and therefore will be successful. One drawback is that, because you lack experience, knowledge, and skills, you often don't know just how little you know. In fact, beginners often think they know a great deal. Overestimating both your knowledge and skills can keep you at the beginner level until you realize what you need to know and how you need to do something. Then you begin to gain the knowledge and skills that move you beyond the beginner level.

Beginners can generally be considered those with less than three years of experience. But more experience alone does not make beginners smarter or more skilled. The sad reality is that some people perform at the beginner level for a lifetime.

Teacher as Beginner

At one time I supervised student teachers in public schools. It was enjoyable because I got to see many bright, enthusiastic young teachers instructing bright, enthusiastic young students. During one visit, the mentor teacher told me he was having a problem with the student teacher. "She shows no respect for my experience," he said. In a meeting together after class, the mentor was quick to air his concerns. The student teacher interjected, "But there are more contemporary ways ... " She was quickly cut off by the mentor's loud proclamation, "I've been teaching for twenty-five years!" The student teacher revealed more pluck than tact when she corrected him, "No. You taught one year and repeated it twenty-four times!" She had a valid point. While the mentor teacher was considered a nice person, few considered him a good teacher. He had learned little from his experience. We quickly transferred the young student teacher to another school. Interestingly, years later she was named her state's teacher of the year.

Beginner Characteristics

Beyond their lack of experience, generally beginners share four common characteristics. Recognizing these characteristics can help you assess your present level of expertise as a beginner and understand what to do to become more expert. It can also help human resource and training personnel, or potential mentors, determine how to help someone move beyond the beginner level. Beginners commonly

- Behave in ways that are rational, procedural, and inflexible
- Make decisions guided by rules and norms
- Do not feel responsible for the outcomes of their actions
- Lack comfortable, efficient routines for everyday tasks

Behaving Rationally, Procedurally, and Inflexibly

As a beginner, with your limited experience, knowledge, and skills, you have few options when it comes to taking action. Limited knowledge and skills provide you with limited options when identifying problems, planning actions, or completing tasks. As a result, you must rely on rational thought rather than on instinct or practical knowledge. As a beginner, you often look for procedures to follow and patterns of behavior to emulate. Lacking a deep understanding as to *why* something may be done in a particular way, you will often simply accept *how* it is done by those who seem to be in the know. Your actions therefore tend to be rigid and step-by-step as you attempt to follow established procedures learned in training programs or by reading manuals.

To help beginners become productive quickly, training instructions often offer a progressive sequence of steps that translate easily into action. Computer maker Hewlett-Packard, for example, offers beginning salespeople a seven-step procedure for selling digital printers:[1]

1. Get in the door.
2. Identify their pain.

3. Use a leadership sales approach.

4. Talk the talk.

5. Ask the right question.

6. Develop your solution.

7. Present the solution.

Tips for implementing each step are also offered. This procedure serves as a recipe for sales success and saves beginning salespeople much time—time that would otherwise be spent on experiments with various techniques and models. The steps are rational and procedural and, because they are sequential, they are also relatively inflexible.

While supplying beginners with rational procedures for accomplishing the fundamental tasks of their profession is an important and useful goal of training programs—and beginners adapting to accepted behavioral practices in their job is smart, profitable politics—serious and detrimental consequences can result if conditions and circumstances are not carefully considered. There are times when following established procedures may not be the best course of action. Ray Alcorn makes this point in his article "Top 5 Mistakes of Beginning Commercial Real Estate Investors" when he identifies the number one mistake beginning investors make as ignoring local market conditions.[2] A beginner often believes that a great property equals a great investment, but as Alcorn notes, "A great property in a bad market can be a big loser. Analyzing the demographic trends of population growth, income, and employment in the local market will tell you where opportunity lies, or not. Those conditions will make or break your investment." In other words, following a rigid set of procedures for all properties in all markets can lead to disaster for beginning investors.

Every organization has tasks for which specific, inflexible procedures work well. For example, completing travel reimbursements, processing orders, and posting organizationwide announcements are conducted more efficiently when everyone follows the same process—regardless of experience, position in the organization, or level of expertise. However,

As beginners, we cannot stay stuck in a rigid approach forever if we want to advance to the next step.

Strictly following traditional procedures helps beginners fit in a new organization, but if they do not explore alternatives, they will remain relatively low-level performers.

Making Decisions Guided by Rules and Norms

When you are a beginner, your decisions usually are tied to the rules and norms of an organization. Rules offer guides to decisions and actions, and norms are the stuff of corporate cultures and traditions. Thus, rules represent the explicit or stated principles on which to make decisions, whereas norms are the implicit or unspoken beliefs and values that shape how people think in a workplace.

To become competent in your new role and prove yourself worthy, as a beginner, you learn the rules and norms that govern behavior in the new workplace. Your conception of doing the job correctly includes decisions based on the workplace rules and traditions, particularly those centered on establishing order and managing the workplace environment. You see established, orderly practices as characteristic of competence.

Rules and norms can provide the foundation for greater understanding and expertise.

Changing Focus

The story of Marvin Traub demonstrates how an individual can learn the rules and norms on which to base decisions in his industry. During his first week at Bloomingdale's, Marvin was called into chairman Jed Davidson's office. Marvin was instructed to analyze the cost of *Daily News* full-color ads and to calculate how much was being lost on Bloomingdale's dresses that were selling for $2.99. (This was in 1950!) Marvin was surprised to learn that Mr. Davidson thought the dresses were losing money, because these particular dresses sold very well. But Jed Davidson was asking, Did it make good business sense? So Marvin added up the wholesale costs of the dresses sold and deducted the cost of advertising. He was shocked by what he found: Bloomingdale's lost twenty-five to thirty-five cents on every dress it sold. The more dresses it sold, the more money it lost. The store gave up the full-page ads, and Marvin learned the first rule of retailing: Focus not on gross sales but on profit! Later, as chairman and CEO, Marvin Traub used that rule to lead Bloomingdale's to a position of celebrated prominence in American retailing.[3]

Genius in a Little Rule

I found a personal example of a foundational rule one evening in Home Depot. A broken toilet had sent me off in search of a replacement part. I walked into the plumbing section with a broken something-or-other. It was only a small piece of a larger part of the entire apparatus.

A young associate greeted me with a smile and a welcome: "How can I help you?" I presented the piece to him. "What is it?" he asked. "I don't know. It came out of my toilet tank," I replied. "Oh, I think we can help you." He then examined several possibilities for a replacement, and when he thought he found one, he confirmed his decision with a colleague. Next, he carefully explained, step-by-step, how to replace the part and assured me that I had all the tools I needed. The entire process took about thirty minutes. The total cost of the part was less than four dollars. Home Depot made no money on my purchase. When I complimented the associate on his excellent customer service, he said that during training he was told that he should "treat every customer like a relative." As we parted, he said, "I would have done the same for any member of my family." There is genius in that simple little rule: *Treat every customer like a relative.* First, it gave that beginner sales professional a clear guide when making customer service decisions. Second, it provided superior service that ensured that I will return many times to a place that treats me like family.

Failing to Take Responsibility for One's Actions

On Friday, August 26, 2005, National Hurricane Center director Max Mayfield reported to the press, "I just don't see any reason why this will not become a very, very powerful hurricane before it is all over."[4] Three days later Hurricane Katrina came out of the Gulf of Mexico and slammed onto shore near the Louisiana–Mississippi state line. A short time later, two major flood control levees were breached, submerging New Orleans. Twelve hours later, one of the most powerful hurricanes in U.S. history was finally downgraded to a tropical storm; but, in Katrina's wake lay death, devastation, and hundreds of thousands of people without food, water, or shelter.

Michael Brown joined the Federal Emergency Management Agency (FEMA) in 2001 as legal counsel. In 2003, he became director. Prior to joining FEMA, he had spent ten years as a commissioner for the International Arabian Horse Association. With no training or experience in emergency management, Michael Brown was a beginner in a position—heading the federal government's emergency management agency—needing an expert.

As is characteristic of beginners, Brown did not feel responsible for the disaster unfolding in New Orleans. He refused to shoulder responsibility for FEMA's slow response to the disaster, and instead blamed Louisiana's leaders for failing to act quickly enough to the approaching hurricane. When informed by a FEMA employee in New Orleans that they were running out of food and water, and that people were dying due to a lack of proper medical facilities, Brown e-mailed back, "Thanks for the update. Anything specific I need to do or tweak?"[5]

As a beginner, you seldom feel you have personal control over conditions and events. That feeling can lead to a lack of a sense of responsibility for the consequences of your actions or inactions. When you fail, you often blame conditions, resources, or others for your failure. "I wasn't trained for this," "That's not my job," or "If we had the same resources as our competitors, we would have won that contract" are thoughts commonly expressed by beginners and others with limited expertise. As a beginner, if you blindly follow the rules, you cannot adequately analyze a problem or see possible solutions that may actually be within your knowledge base or skill set. If you've followed procedures and made decisions guided by the rules and tradition, you may feel you've done all that can reasonably be expected and become a passive participant in the process.

Taking Responsibility

In a recent study, twenty-one ultraendurance triathletes were divided by finishing times into three groups: leaders of the pack, middle of the pack, and back of the pack. The triathletes' decision making during their performance was analyzed, and the findings are startling. The leaders focused tightly on actions to improve their performance, whereas middle- and back-of-the-pack triathletes reported a greater number of passive thoughts. For example, middle-of-the-packers might passively observe that it was a warm day, whereas leaders would consider how the temperature might impact their performance and subsequently make adjustments in their pace, nutrition, equipment, and hydration. Furthermore, leaders were more proactive in their approach to performance situations than were middle- and back-of-the-pack triathletes. They saw their performance as a direct result of their actions and took proactive responsibility. The lower performers felt no such responsibility and consequently were proactive in neither decisions nor actions.[6]

As a beginner, you may feel a lack of control and responsibility. If so, you may not be inclined to put much effort toward improving your performance when you feel you have neither responsibility for nor control of the results. You may even dismiss poor performance as normal and acceptable and give up early and easily. This characteristic is a watershed mark in developing expertise. When you feel responsible for outcomes and adjust your actions to improve your performance, you begin moving to the next step toward becoming expert.

Whereas beginners may give up on clients, products, or plans too quickly, superior performers are never willing to give up.

The drive to succeed and reach their full potential propels great leaders, inventors, writers, and entrepreneurs to the pinnacle of their profession. Should you ever find yourself giving up on a business matter, realize that you are also giving up on yourself as a businessperson.

Refusing to give up and searching for ways to turn defeat to victory help move you past the beginner step.

Lacking Comfortable, Efficient Routines

Beginners sometimes become mired in the mundane because they haven't established personal work routines. They don't have the ability to see the interconnection of events in a business. A beginning sales representative may, for example, get caught up in friendly communications with a potential customer while overlooking more important tasks such as closing a sale, taking an order, or scheduling a delivery.

It's hard for beginners to sense the overall objective or see the relationships between events. The bigger picture that includes what came before and what will likely happen later eludes you as you concentrate solely on the immediate challenge before you. Which challenges or tasks are unique and which will repeat over time are a mystery, so every task is approached as a new challenge every time.

With increased experience and discussions with colleagues, beginners start to recognize consistencies in the everyday or mundane activities of the workday.

As consistent activities recur, you start to develop effective routines to minimize organizational and management functions so that you can maximize your focus on completing the most essential tasks effectively. These routines are based on increased experience, knowledge, and skills, as well as familiarity, in the workplace. Through trial and error you find not only what works but also what feels comfortable. Being provided with examples and alternatives for conducting the activities of a business can help you select and cultivate those routines that increase both the quality and the quantity of your work.

How Beginners Learn

It's possible to remain a beginner for a lifetime. To move to the next level of expertise, you need to gain experience, to increase knowledge, and to develop some useful skills. Beginners have three preferred ways of learning:

- From experience
- With guidance from rules and established procedures
- Through mentoring

Experience: The Greatest Teacher

For beginners, few things beat trial and error (especially error) for learning. Despite anything you're told, you just have to go out and see for yourself how things are. Perhaps reflecting your limited practical experience, real-world practice is your most important source of information for increasing competence. For beginners acquiring knowledge and skills, verbal or written information almost always takes second place to trial and error.

Simply put, there is no substitute for experience. Beginners usually develop a repertoire of professional skills by combining observations of experienced colleagues, personal trial-and-error experiences, and recollections of early role models. The more experiences and the greater the diversity of those experiences, the faster beginners learn and the more they improve. However, while experience is a critical aspect of improving performance, experience alone does not increase expertise.

Rules and Established Procedures: Important

For organizations, having a clear set of written rules and established procedures—all consistently applied—can prove enormously useful to beginners in steering their decisions and actions during their first years on the job.

If you were a new employee at Monster Cable Products, Inc., for example, on your first day you would be handed a single laminated sheet called Monster Mottos. These are the company's operating principles and procedures as spelled out by visionary founder and head monster Dr. Noel Lee. Here is a sampling of the headings and some of the entries under each:

- Monsterous Business Strategy (Sooner is better than later.)
- Monsterous Personal Skills (Do what you say you are going to do within the time you say you are going to do it.)
- Monsterous Judgment (Find out what you don't know, that is, the root cause: Don't just treat the symptom; cure the disease.)

Mentoring: Invaluable

Among a journalist's first assignments was covering city council meetings. What did she know about the city council or its meetings? Nothing. So what did she do? She was smart enough to know if she just plowed her way ignorantly through the assignment, she could miss something and her report would be neither accurate nor newsworthy. Rather than quietly taking a seat at the back of the room like many beginners would, she "walked into the city council meeting and announced to everybody there, 'This is my first day on the job, and I don't know anything. Please help me.' And they did."[7]

It is uncharacteristic for beginners to ask for help. No one likes to admit ignorance. But the cub reporter asked those with experience for help—and got it. She did not remain a beginner for long. In fact, that reporter went on to become one of the most successful individuals in broadcast history. No one would have known her on that first assignment; but today, Oprah Winfrey is one of the most familiar faces on television.

As a beginning reporter, Winfrey realized that the importance of guidance and demonstrations from experienced professionals cannot be overstated. If we can't learn by doing, we can learn by observing. On the other hand, learning by listening is not a high-impact learning strategy for beginners: People need to be shown how it is done, not told. A good mentor has a longer-lasting effect on a person than any training manual or lecture. So, beginners who have not "been there, done that" should find people who have and learn from their experiences.

Going Beyond Beginner

You need to do more than just spend time on the job to become more skilled. You need to learn from your experiences and gain a great deal more knowledge to reduce mistakes and increase successes. Combining experience with activities such as reflective practice, journal writing, professional meetings, reading, and networking with colleagues can help beginners gain knowledge and insight. This purposeful and sustained effort to improve increases your level of expertise—nothing less. When you work deliberately to learn from experience, gain more knowledge, and improve your skills, you do not remain a beginner for long.

In the next chapter, the characteristics that signal the rise from beginner to capable performer are identified and described. Prepare to take that step by completing expertise exercises 5–7.

Summary

Beginner performers

- Behave in ways that are rational, procedural, and inflexible
- Make decisions guided by rules and norms
- Do not feel responsible for the outcomes of their actions
- Lack comfortable, efficient routines for everday tasks

EXPERTISE EXERCISE 5

IDENTIFYING RULES TO LIVE BY

Identify workplace or professional rules to live by that you might write for beginners in your workplace.

Rules to live by at

_____

(your organization)

1. _____

2. _____

3. _____

4. _____

5. _____

LEARNING FROM EXPERIENCE

Identify a recent experience you will likely encounter again in the near future. What will you do differently in the future that you did not do in the past to improve your efficiency, effectiveness, or performance?

_____

_____

_____

_____

_____

_____

_____

_____

_____

_____

_____

_____

_____

_____

_____

_____

_____

_____

MEETING MENTORS

Identify someone or some people in your workplace you would consider approaching as a mentor. Identify the characteristics and skills they possess that you would most like to possess as well.

Person 1: _____

    Characteristics: _____

    _____

    _____

    Skills: _____

    _____

Person 2: _____

    Characteristics: _____

    _____

    _____

    Skills: _____

    _____

Person 3: _____

    Characteristics: _____

    _____

    _____

    Skills: _____

    _____

THREE

CONVERTING TO CAPABLE

With a few years' experience, increased knowledge, and the development of some basic skills, you begin making the conversion from beginner to capable. When you are capable, you get the job done. For beginners, getting the job done can be a hit-or-miss proposition: Sometimes they do and sometimes they don't. Someone who is capable is far more consistent and efficient in completing assigned tasks and handling responsibilities. Decisions are made a bit faster, refined skills lead to better outcomes, procedures are executed smoothly, and transitions from one task to another are made more quickly. These are all signs of a capable performer.

In his book *Good to Great*, Jim Collins defines the level-one (first level) executive as a "highly capable individual [who] makes productive contributions through talent, knowledge, skills, and good work habits."[1] People at the capable level of expertise generally

- Have functional skills and focus on task requirements
- See similarities across contexts
- Can make decisions in a timely manner

- Are responsive to situations
- Use strategic knowledge in decision making
- Learn best from experience but develop other resources as well

Having Functional Skills and Focusing on Task Requirements

The management team at Cabela's, one of the largest retailers of outdoor equipment in the United States, faced a mountain of challenges as it prepared to open a 175,000-square-foot megastore in Wheeling, West Virginia, in August 2004. Finding people to fill the four hundred frontline positions was high among those challenges. The criteria for selecting those who would be on the sales floor were clearly articulated by manager Tony Gatti: "You give me somebody who's dedicated and has a love and a passion for the outdoors, and I can teach him what he needs to know about retail."[2] In other words, beginners could be taught the functional retail skills to make them capable salespeople if they possessed experience, knowledge, and skills in the core industry—the outdoors.

When you perform a task or job on the capable level, you get the job done with serviceable skills; that is, the level of skill is adequate for the requirements of the task, but not extraordinary. Cabela's is clearly not the only business that relies on functional skills from certain employees. Many positions in business require only functional skills. Assembly-line workers, for example, are required to repeat the same skill again and again and again with a degree of both speed and accuracy. Most employees in the fast-food industry are required to have functional skills. As long as the skills are executed so as to complete the required task within acceptable standards, the job done is considered satisfactory. Capable employees who execute functional skills do so with consistency, which is critical to quality control. Because those with functional skills command a lower wage than those with more developed skills, these individuals are critical to cost control.

On most assembly lines, seldom is one worker identified as more skilled than another. All that is required of these employees is a capable level of performance. Because skills cannot be differentiated, experience is normally the primary determiner of wage standards (that is, those with more experience receive a greater wage). Training for such a position often extends no further than ensuring that the employee can perform a task or tasks to the required standard. Functional skills are not solely the domain of the blue-collar worker. Many such skills are found in every profession or occupation—and at every level.

Unlike beginners, capable performers have some relevant experience. When you have some level of experience in a workplace, you move beyond simply following procedures when undertaking tasks, but you still maintain a tight focus on meeting the job requirements rather than focusing on the purpose or quality of your performance. An example of this level of focus was revealed in a research investigation of forty professional software designers.[3] Highly rated performers undertook their designs with a focus on planning and results, whereas capable performers focused on analyzing the task requirements and verbalizing task-irrelevant thoughts. Interestingly, highly and moderately rated performers did not differ with respect to length of experience.

The skills of a capable performer are focused on adequately meeting the task or job requirements—nothing more, nothing less.

Seeing Similarities Across Contexts

Edwin Land, founder of Polaroid and holder of more than five hundred U.S. patents, understood well the importance of capable individuals seeing and connecting similarities across contexts. In telling a story about how color film was invented, he spotlighted the benefit of that ability. He wrote,

> When I started on the actual program of making the black-and-white film for our camera, I set down broad principles that would also apply to color. I invited Howard Rogers, who had worked with me for many years in the field of polarized light, to sit opposite me in the black-and-white laboratory and think about color. For several years he simply sat and, saying very little, assimilated the techniques we were using in black-and-white. Then one day he stood up and said, "I'm ready to start now." So we built him the color laboratory next to the black-and-white laboratory.[4]

Over time, recurring events in the workplace are recognized and remembered. When the unfamiliar becomes familiar, knowledge of situations, people, and activities expands and deepens, and you can envision similarities across contexts. Being able to identify these similiarities, you can select an appropriate solution from those tested during prior experiences. Increased expertise emerges when you examine a new experience by searching for a solution or decision from previous experiences rather than relying strictly on established rules or prescribed procedures as you did when you were a beginner.

Insight into similarities across contexts was first revealed in a classic study in 1981 by University of Pittsburgh researchers Michelene Chi, Paul Feltovich, and Robert Glaser. Physicists were given a series of problems and then asked to sort the problems and analyze the nature of their groupings. The scientists with more expertise used principles of mechanics to categorize the problems, while those with less expertise used literal factors stated in the problem description to categorize the problems. The research team concluded that those with more expertise "are able to 'see' the underlying similarities in a great number of problems, whereas the novices 'see' a variety of problems that they consider to be dissimilar because the surface features are different."[5]

Capable individuals with more expertise classify problems based on principles; beginners see problems based on surface features.

This study suggests that to fully understand the nature of a problem, you must identify principles and similarities the current problem shares with previous problems. While this ability becomes highly developed in elite performers, it begins to emerge as you leave the beginner level and enter the capable level of expertise.

Because you recognize similarities across situations, you can make applications from one situation to another. This was a principle Sam Walton embraced when he was first starting out as a retailer. With a yellow legal pad or a tape recorder, he marched into every competitor's store he could find. He was seeking information about pricing, displays, and how competitors' businesses were run. He brought back the lessons he learned to Wal-Mart and applied the lessons that fit with similar situations in his stores. According to Walton, "We're really not concerned with what competitors are doing wrong; we're concerned with what they are doing right."[6] Few discount retailers would argue whether Sam Walton got it right.

Making Decisions in a Timely Manner

Time-pressured situations call especially for the application of expertise. An offshore oil rig can be a dangerous place to work. With large amounts of heavy and sophisticated equipment attended to by a small army, and all perched precariously over an ever-changing sea miles from dry land or help, the decisions made on the oil rig have serious and immediate consequences. A single mistake can quickly translate to a catastrophic disaster.

Researchers studied the decision making of eighteen offshore oil rig managers from two operating companies. In simulated emergencies, they found all of the managers could identify the first critical decisions to be made, as well as the cues, goals, and expectations for handling the emergency. They were all well trained. The decision-making responses of the most experienced managers, however, showed something a bit different from the rest. The seasoned veterans had recognition-based principles in place for managing emergencies. In other words, they used carefully considered criteria to determine the significance of the events unfolding; and, then, after they recognized the critical factors, they initiated previously tested solutions to handle the situation. With their experience, they were able to see similarities across the events that potentially could lead to disaster. They not only saw the similarities; they also were prepared to respond in ways that prevented catastrophe.[7]

Time is a luxury you do not have in situations where an action must be taken *now!* Research also has shown that the classical decision-making model guided by a rational thought process is not always used by those with more expertise to make decisions.[8] In situations and environments where time is of the essence, experts often trade decision accuracy for decision speed. The rational decision-making process requiring rich resources and careful consideration of multiple options is not effective in urgent situations.

Capable individuals in time-pressured situations typically look for patterns in the situational cues. When you see the features of the events unfolding now as similar to those of events you previously experienced, you can make decisions based on the decisions made in those previous, similar situations. These recognition-primed decisions and actions do not require a great deal of time or thought to achieve acceptable results and have the added benefit of reducing your vulnerability to the stress imposed by time pressure.

Being Responsive to Situations

He had put in close to seventy hours that week knocking on front doors in small villages and farms in northern Indiana trying to sell books. For his efforts, Aaron Meyers made about sixty cents an hour. Minimum wage at the time was $1.25. Something had to change. He was wearing the skin off his knuckles pounding on doors, but people were not listening to his sales pitch. He was following rules and procedures but not getting the results. So Aaron tried something different: He began asking questions. When a potential customer would respond with a reason for not buying a book, Aaron would say, "I understand." He would then ask a couple of questions: "Wouldn't we have loved to have books like these in our home when we were kids?" and "If your children asked you the difference between a verb and an adverb, wouldn't you like to have a book like this to show them the difference?" He got his customers to talk. Specifically, he got his customers to talk *themselves* into the sale. Rather than strictly following the rules for pitching his books, Aaron was responding to the situation and his customers. His sales quickly began to climb as he became a capable sales professional. But he didn't stop developing sales skills or learning more about situations and customers. As the International Division president of the Tom James Clothing Company, the world's largest retailer of custom clothing, Aaron Meyers continues to learn today so he can find more success tomorrow.

Where beginners rely on rules and procedures to guide virtually all their actions, capable individuals let situations, in part, guide their actions and decisions.

You are capable when you realize that not every rule applies in every situation.

Rules and procedures remain useful, but decisions and actions become more responsive to the nuances and subtleties of a situation. For example, if hiring managers strictly follow a rule that they can hire only people with an appropriate and accredited college degree, they may miss the opportunity to hire an individual of exceptional competence and knowledge of the field. Albert Einstein's academic degrees were revoked by the Nazis in the 1930s, and Bill Gates has yet to complete his Harvard undergraduate degree. Does that mean the rule of hiring only those with a college degree is inadequate? Not necessarily. But there may be situations in which the application of the rule is counterproductive to the goals of the organization or person.

Breaking the Rules

Dr. Rita Levi-Montalcini graduated summa cum laude in 1936 from the University of Turin Medical School. Just three years later, she was forced out of her research position by a Fascist law forbidding Jews to work in academic or professional fields. With the threat of arrest and deportation by the Nazis, her family went into hiding. While the rules forbade her to conduct research, she was not to be deterred. She built a small research laboratory in her bedroom to continue her study of neurological development in chick embryos. Heavy Allied bombing soon forced her to move into the country. She built another laboratory and resumed her experiments. She scoured the countryside, where food was scarce, for fertilized eggs for her research. Frequent power outages shut off the incubator that was used to grow the embryos, often destroying weeks of work. Levi-Montalcini broke the rules, endured, and prevailed. In 1986, she was awarded a Nobel Prize for her nerve growth research that now helps combat dementia, tumors, and muscular dystrophy.[9] Had she not responded, and broken the rules, the world today clearly would be a poorer place.

To develop this characteristic, people must understand what needs to be done to reach the ultimate outcome and work within the immediate demands of the workplace. Beginners are still learning the fundamentals of the business and may be unable to see clearly the final result of their actions. Capable individuals with some experience and knowledge of the workplace understand the situation in which they find themselves and then take a course of action that achieves the desired outcome.

Using Strategic Knowledge in Decision Making

A ticket agent in Minneapolis, on a wintry February Friday, cemented my loyalty to her airline. As I checked in at the gate for my late afternoon flight to Atlanta, the ticket agent informed me that there was room on an earlier flight to my home city. With a snowstorm moving in, she offered to put me on at no charge to ensure that I made it home for the weekend. The airline's charge for changing a ticket was $100. Needless to say, when it comes to future flight reservations, I will look to that airline, whose capable professionals use strategic knowledge in the best interests of their customers and, ultimately, their company.

When you are capable, you have an advantage over beginners in the area of experience. As you accumulate experience, you begin cataloging recurring events and problems, which leads to seeing similarities across contexts. But your experience also provides you with knowledge of the consequences of your previous actions. When a problem presents itself, you can recall similar, previously solved problems for help in understanding which actions will lead to which outcomes.

> **Capable performers use strategic knowledge by taking action based on knowledge of the consequences of previous actions.**

According to researchers Ann Graham and Vincent Pizzo, in the business world "understanding the business battleground, be it product or service dimensions (e.g., costs, precision, value, quality) or environmental factors (e.g., competitive forces, regulations, socio-economic trends), is a logical starting point for deciding how to organize and manage knowledge assets."[10] Because you have faced similar challenges and gained an understanding of the business battleground, you can better understand the long-term consequences of your actions. For example, something you did in a given situation may have solved the immediate problem but had long-term negative consequences. You have also acted in ways that not only solved the immediate problem but also prevented future problems and had long-term positive consequences. When the ticket agent moved me to that earlier flight, she took care of her immediate responsibility of getting me on a plane to Atlanta. The long-term consequence of bending that rebooking rule was that not only did she avoid having to find me a seat on a flight the next day if my original flight were canceled due to the storm, but she also gained a loyal customer for her company. A beginner would have strictly followed the rules and made life difficult for both me and possibly the airline.

By using strategic knowledge, as a capable person you are in a position to solve multiple problems and handle several tasks simultaneously. When you use strategic knowledge, you select actions that provide multiple benefits or consequences in a given situation. Beginners may solve the immediate problem with little understanding of the long-term consequences of their actions. In a study of sales professionals, for example, the more capable salespeople had a deeper knowledge of both their customers' traits and effective sales strategies. Thus, they developed more sophisticated sales scripts that accommodated a wider range of both traits and strategies than did the less capable sales professionals.[11]

As a capable performer, you may still be somewhat rule oriented, but now circumstances and context can guide you in how to apply the rules and in knowing when to ignore or flex the rules as the situation dictates. Flexibility in following rules was observed in a recent study of physicians' decisions when they prescribe drugs. The study found that physicians with more experience in drug therapy were more idiosyncratic in prescribing drugs than physicians with less experience. Although both groups followed the prescription guidelines for each drug, those with more experience were more strategic in prescribing drugs because they saw the therapy in more holistic terms and adapted prescriptions to the individual patient. Junior physicians were more formulaic and rule-bound in their approach. This study suggests that it may be as important to know when to depart from standard medical practice as it is to know the standards of medical practice. Capable physicians develop strategic knowledge to guide their medical decision making.[12]

Strategic knowledge is incubated in experience and fed knowledge that is pertinent to accomplishing specific tasks. It grows from trial and error, tapping into knowledge sources and recognizing similarities in events. Developing this knowledge requires that you

- Acquire experience
- Reflect on decisions and actions to learn all you can from each experience
- Experiment with viable alternatives to repetitive tasks associated with your job

- See a variety of sources for helpful information (reading, talking with colleagues, observing others in action, etc.)

The greater your ability to leverage strategic knowledge in making decisions and taking action, the greater the gains you make toward becoming expert.

Developing Other Learning Resources

Experience taught you well when you were a beginner, and it continues as your teacher when you are a capable performer. However, experience alone won't teach you all you seek to know. Capable performers therefore begin looking to sources outside their immediate circle of daily activities for new information to solve old problems, increase performance efficiency, or discover an innovative practice.

Capable performers find accomplished colleagues particularly valuable.

A host of factors inhibit beginners from depending on colleagues as an information source, including an unwillingness to admit a lack of knowledge or skills, a belief that colleagues don't know any more than they do, and a self-directed orientation—rather than a team or goal orientation—to every problem. With gains in experience and increased knowledge of both the work and the workplace, you develop relationships with colleagues and feel comfortable asking for help or an opinion without the fear of being thought incompetent. You also realize that others in the workplace are both knowledgeable and willing to help.

From the *Journal of Applied Business Research* comes a study on the performance of middle managers.[13] Middle managers achieve varying levels of success based on strategies they use in undertaking projects. The most successful managers—"leaders" in the study—integrate their skills and expertise with that of colleagues through both formal and informal interactions. In their work, they not only are willing to lend their knowledge and skills to others but are also comfortable asking their colleagues for support in areas where they may lack expertise.

The least successful managers—"laggards" in the study—had the necessary skills and knowledge for success but were unable to mobilize the necessary social support network to shore up limitations or weaknesses. The point is this: The differences between middle managers who lead and those who lag are not found in experience, knowledge, or skills, but rather in the ability to utilize help from capable colleagues.

Interestingly, as you gain expertise, the fear of being perceived as incompetent fades. Experts seldom shy away from asking for needed help—even if the person who may be able to help them is a rank beginner who just happens to know something the expert does not. A new employee, for example, may have extensive knowledge of Web design and navigation. Experts in business are not necessarily expert in using the Internet, but they will quickly make use of their new colleagues with such expertise. Comfort in asking for help first begins to reveal itself at the capable level.

In addition to continued experience and depending on colleagues, capable people become aware of areas of strengths and weaknesses in their professional practice. They are learning to leverage their strengths, but at this stage they also realize they must shore up their shortcomings. To that end capable individuals may seek out varied sources of knowledge that help them to overcome their deficiencies. Books, journals, training programs, observing others, and so forth are tapped from time to time as knowledge sources. You may not realize just how rich these resources are for new knowledge until much later in your development. But, as a capable performer, you begin to make that discovery.

Moving Toward Competence

In many businesses being capable is sufficient, and you may find neither personal nor professional motivation to develop further. If being good enough is just not good enough for you, however, then you are likely to become more expert. If you are motivated to stretch your experience, increase your knowledge, and gain greater skills in executing professional actions, you may find several learning strategies that are especially helpful in climbing to the competent level—your next step toward becoming expert.

As you continue to increase your experience, knowledge, and deliberate practice of professional skills, your capable characteristics soon give way to characteristics that accompany the next step toward expertise: competence. Expertise exercises 8–10 can help further your development.

Summary

Capable performers

- Have functional skills and focus on task requirements
- See similarities across contexts
- Can make decisions in a timely manner
- Are responsive to situations
- Use strategic knowledge in decision making
- Learn best from experience but develop other resources as well

EXPERTISE EXERCISE 8

RESPONDING TO SITUATIONS

There are times when a capable performer gains a better result by responding to a situation rather than strictly following established rules. Recall a situation in which you found the rules of your organization inadequate for achieving a superior outcome. Describe the situation, the rule, and what you did (or speculate on what you might have done) rather than strictly following that rule in order to achieve a better outcome.

_____

_____

_____

_____

_____

EXPERTISE EXERCISE 9

DEVELOPING STRATEGIC KNOWLEDGE

Capable individuals develop strategic knowledge, allowing them to ignore or flex rules or policies in certain situations. Recall a recent workplace event where you used strategic knowledge instead of a rule or policy. Was the outcome more positive or less positive than if you had followed the rule or policy? Explain.

_____

_____

_____

_____

_____

MAXIMIZING RESOURCES

Describe some accessible resources that will increase your workplace performance. This might include registering for a seminar or class, reading a relevant book (e.g., a biography, self-help book, or how-to manual), or bookmarking a Web site that you can visit regularly for fresh information about your current, or future, job responsibilities.

1. _____

2. _____

3. _____

4. _____

5. _____

FOUR

CULTIVATING COMPETENCE

When increases in knowledge and skills are combined with experiences accumulated as a capable performer, competence is cultivated. Competent performers not only get the job done—they get it done well. They are good at what they do, and people recognize them for their experience, knowledge, and skills. Competent performers commonly

- Use goals and long-term plans to guide decisions and actions
- Distinguish important from unimportant factors when analyzing situations or events
- Plan contingently
- Have a sense of timing and momentum in making decisions and taking actions

The majority of people in any organization are usually competent. To do a job well on a consistent basis normally satisfies the boss, the clients, and other stakeholders. If the majority of people in an organization are not at least competent, the business is likely to languish, if not outright fail. It is therefore in the best interest of any organization to ensure that its people are provided the opportunity, experience, and education to become better at what they do. It is also incumbent on an organization to hire those people who are committed to becoming at least competent in executing the duties and obligations of their position. The level of competence for people in that organization is not only a direct reflection of the organization but also of them as individuals.

If you are not committed to becoming competent, or beyond, there is little chance you will succeed in your business.

If that is the case, perhaps it's time to find another business you can take pride in and have passion for.

It would be easy to think that the point in bold type above is a hollow motivational pitch. Far from it. It is part of the formula for success—yours, as well as your organization's. This point is best exemplified by one of the most successful airlines in the skies today—Southwest Airlines—on its Web site:

The Mission of Southwest Airlines
The mission of Southwest Airlines is dedication to the highest quality of Customer Service delivered with a sense of warmth, friendliness, individual pride, and Company Spirit.

To Our Employees
We are committed to provide our Employees a stable work environment with equal opportunity for learning and personal growth. Creativity and innovation are encouraged for improving the effectiveness of Southwest Airlines. Above all, Employees will be provided the same concern, respect, and caring attitude within the organization that they are expected to share externally with every Southwest Customer.[1]

The Southwest mission statement clearly reflects the belief that the success of an organization is dependent on its people's competence, and the competence of its people is clearly dependent on the organization. Make no mistake: Southwest Airlines has been successful. Its net profit margins have been the highest in the airline industry. From 1990 to 1996, its stock price rose 300 percent.[2]

As you learn more about the tasks to be completed and gain experience in accomplishing them, you begin to develop skills that allow you to perform with efficiency and effectiveness. At this level of expertise, you have a firm grasp on the tasks that pattern your daily business life, feel relatively comfortable in your working environment, and, for the most part, make people happy with your performance. And why shouldn't they be? You are competent and can get the job done!

You're competent because you now possess certain characteristics that you didn't have when you were a beginner or a capable performer. These characteristics contribute to your ability to undertake tasks and responsibilities with greater and more consistent success. Realize that they are cues signaling your ascension from the lower levels of expertise. Developing these characteristics enabled you to elevate your level of expertise, and continuing to cultivate them will maintain your level of competence and perhaps elevate it higher.

Using Goals and Long-Term Plans to
Guide Decisions and Actions

Shortly after the D-day invasion of France in World War II, Winston Churchill, the British prime minister, disagreed with the other Allied leaders about next steps. President Roosevelt wanted a follow-up invasion on the southern coast of France, whereas Churchill believed a stronger push in Italy was a better use of resources. After a long and heated discussion with Army General Alan Brooke, Churchill recognized that, in the bigger scheme of the war, it was better to have a strong bond with his allies than to win every point of disagreement. He therefore gave his consent to Roosevelt and informed General Brooke, "All right, if you insist on being damned fools, sooner than falling out with you, which would be fatal, we shall be damned fools with you, and we shall see that we perform the role of damned fools damned well!"[3]

Where beginners struggle to apply the rules and handle the immediate challenges, competent people long ago mastered the rules and are comfortable with the everyday challenges of their job. Rather than being absorbed by the immediate and mundane demands of the workplace, those who are competent work toward broader goals to ensure long-term success.

The practices of competent professionals are guided more by purpose than by policies and procedures.

In describing the elements of decision making by effective executives, Peter Drucker identified the first question the effective decision maker asks: "Is this a generic situation or an exception?"[4] Is the cause of the situation something that underlies many occurrences, or is the cause unique to this particular event? Only in seeing the bigger picture do executives know if the situation is caused by a long-term problem or a blip in the process. If the situation is long-term and part of the bigger picture, then the decision must be one in which a principle is engaged and applied. The principle should support the long-term health and welfare of the organization, because making a series of temporary decisions is akin to putting your finger in a crumbling dike.

Competent performers also have a greater ability to plan. They possess the knowledge and skills to anticipate events, to adjust for changes in those events, and to implement plans to guide decisions and actions. This level of thinking and acting is beyond the abilities of most beginners and capable performers because they lack the experience, knowledge, and skills of a competent performer.[5]

Competent performers gain several advantages when they focus more on long-term goals rather than on near-term tasks. First, with the strategic knowledge gained as a capable performer, the competent performer knows the likely consequences of potential reaction. Selecting actions to meet long-term goals thus becomes easier. Second, with a long-term goal in mind, the competent performer is able to prioritize which tasks and strategies are most crucial in meeting the goal. Third, knowing the long-term goal and the tasks and actions that most likely lead to achieving the goal, the competent performer is able to be more judicious in resource allocation: Resources such as time, attention, and supplies can be dedicated to those actions that have the highest likelihood of accomplishing the objective.[6]

In a study comparing the planning of expert and beginner basketball coaches, several striking distinctions were discovered.[7] Experts focused more attention on information cues about player skill levels, abilities, and personal traits than did the beginner coaches. Consequently, the experts were more deliberate planners, requiring 60 percent more time to plan than beginners. Experts focused more attention than beginners did on establishing objectives for practice sessions and then developing activities to achieve the objectives as well as strategies for evaluating the attainment of objectives. An analysis of the experts' goal structures indicated that they knew many more routines and alternatives than did the beginners. Also, due to their extensive knowledge, the experts were more confident that their plans would be successful.

To cultivate competence, you must continually revisit the purposes behind your actions. If your only purpose is to maintain the status quo, complete a task, or just get through the day, you are mired in a beginner's perspective. If, however, your purpose is to think several steps ahead so that your efforts amount to something cumulative, a characteristic of competence is evident. Competent people rely on long-term goals and plans to ensure that their efforts work toward the bigger picture of progress and success. Stephen Covey describes this characteristic as follows: "By keeping the end clearly in mind, you can make certain that whatever you do on any particular day does not violate the criteria you have defined as supremely important, and that each day of your life contributes in a meaningful way to the vision you have of your life as a whole."[8] In short, competent people have a clear purpose for doing what they do.

Distinguishing the Important from the Unimportant

Marion O'Brien Donovan is hardly a household name. Few people today, however, are unaffected by a solution she saw in 1946. In the middle of the night, and for the second time that night, she was dealing with a crying baby. The problem she faced was as messy as it was common: a wet diaper, wet bedding, wet clothes—and a wet, uncomfortable, unhappy infant. She was desperate for a solution to this recurring and exhausting problem. Seeing the shower curtain in her bathroom sparked an idea. She tore the curtain down and carried it to her sewing machine, where she fashioned a custom-fitted, leak-proof, reusable diaper cover for her baby. She called her invention the "boater." Her invention was so popular that she soon became a millionaire. As an inventor, she found new ways of using common household items to solve common household problems. Donovan saw the same things in her household that everyone else saw in theirs. She just perceived them differently.[9]

At the competent level, you are able to sort the important from the unimportant. For example, in the same meeting a beginner may notice the dress, writing instruments, or accents of those seated across the table, whereas you, the competent professional, overlook factors that don't bear directly on the intended outcome of the meeting. Instead, you locate the prime decision maker across the table and observe the keen interest she takes in the numbers and the bottom line with seemingly little regard for hypothetical discussions or speculation. During the break, you discover that she attended a well-regarded college and majored in accounting. Your astute perception of several important details has now provided you with valuable insight into the type of information necessary to secure a future with this client, while the beginner is left hoping things went well and wondering where to find an outfit like the one the decision maker was wearing.

The advantages of being able to distinguish the important from the unimportant in a situation should be obvious. This skill enables you to focus on those things that most likely will lead to decisions and actions that will most effectively realize your intended goal. But how do you learn to separate the useful from the useless? The simple answer is that your substantive workplace experience and broad knowledge of the factors that influence workplace performance are key elements in developing this skill. Research, however, has given us two helpful insights into how those with higher levels of expertise can distinguish the important from the unimportant: utility and principles.

Tennis Lessons

A study of tennis instructors with varying levels of expertise revealed no differences in the quantity of cues detected in the instructional environment. Put another way, there was no difference in *how much* information the teachers gathered from their observations. There were, however, substantial differences in *what* they saw. Those with lower levels of expertise identified a range of environmental factors, from what participants wore to where cars were parked. Those with higher levels of expertise saw a different set of factors in the environment. Specifically, they identified principles related to the performance, and from that they were able to locate cues that could be used in helping the performer improve. In other words, they were able to distinguish between the important and the unimportant factors in the environment by recognizing principles accounting for performance and identifying utilitarian information that would prove useful in taking performance-improving action.[10] The difference between important and unimportant information for the more expert teachers was found in the way that information was used for taking effective action.

> In business, if you are competent, in addition to utility you will likely use performance-related principles to sift the important factors from the unimportant.

Programming Abstractly Versus Concretely

The ability of competent performers to focus on more pertinent information was made clear in a study by Yale University professor Beth Adelson. Adelson gave computer programmers a series of tasks that required them to use both abstract and concrete representations of the tasks. She found the thought processes of the more expert programmers were more abstract and contained more general information about what the program did, whereas the beginners' thought processes were more concrete and focused on specific information about how the program functioned. She concluded that "experts have learned that, during comprehension of this type of program, paying attention to the abstract elements of the program is more important than paying attention to the low-level details."[11] By seeing the program as a set of abstract principles, competent programmers do not get bogged down in details but rather focus on the principles to find optimal solutions to problems.

Selectivity is another way to think about this critical attribute of competence. When you have developed the skill of selectivity, you have developed the ability to select those environmental factors that will alter events or can be exploited to manipulate events. You can distinguish the important features from the unimportant in your business landscape.

Planning Contingently

Two key differences emerged in a study of more expert and less expert pilots.[12] First, the more expert pilots spent significantly more time planning and preparing for a flight than did beginners. Second, competent pilots devoted greater effort to gathering the necessary information to plan for the contingencies that would ensure a successful flight. Third, beginners described themselves as passive recipients of information, whereas experts emphasized their active role in seeking information.

Like pilots, those with less business expertise passively, and heavily, rely on procedures and preplanning when conducting business. In contrast, competent businesspeople add another dimension—called contingency, or if-then, planning—that makes them more responsive to unanticipated events or shifting conditions when conducting business.

When planning for an upcoming meeting or program, competent businesspeople are able to plan for contingencies and changes through if-then planning.

For example, a competent salesperson might think something like the following: *If* the client looks interested, *then* I'll spend more time explaining the product. *If* the client looks disinterested in the explanation, *then* I'll go immediately into the demonstration. Again, experience enables you to notice similarities across contexts and provides you with the knowledge to offer a variety of alternatives depending on the situation.

In its early years, the Wm. Wrigley Jr. Company of Chicago sold baking powder. To boost sales, the young owner of the company offered free chewing gum to anyone who bought his baking powder. At the time, chewing gum was an uncertain product in an unproven market. Much to Wrigley's surprise, his dealers began asking if they could order the chewing gum without the baking powder. If they want to buy chewing gum, then I will sell them chewing gum, thought the budding entrepreneur. Now, almost two hundred years later, Wrigley's Spearmint, Juicy Fruit, and Doublemint gums are still in demand.[13]

Contingency planning provides alternatives, and it also makes decision making more fluid. Rather than scripting a series of events and then attempting to follow the script (as a beginner would), competent performers are prepared to make "in-flight" changes to their plans. What fate would have befallen the Wrigley company if its founder had steadfastly believed, "We are a baking powder company"? When you are at the competent level, you realize that no situation ever goes exactly as anticipated, so you are prepared to make adjustments as situations demand and as opportunities arise.

Competent business professionals are goal oriented, which establishes their direction, and their contingency plans help them negotiate the bumps in the road they encounter, as well as seize unexpected opportunities when they arise. Knowledge of their business environment helps them recognize anomalies and opportunities, and their increasing skills enable them to respond in ways that make success likely. Contingency planning bridges knowledge and skills, and converts any business event into a dynamic opportunity for success.

Using Timing and Momentum in Making Decisions and Taking Actions

With the increased experience, knowledge, and skills that raise you to the competent level of expertise, you discover that the order and rhythm of your actions often can make or break an important business event. Accompanying a deeper understanding of the business landscape is the realization that the events unfolding are linked sequentially. That is, they have a history, are influenced by the people and current circumstances, and will affect the events that follow. To influence those events, you must learn to time your decisions and actions to have maximum impact and achieve a successful result.

As a beginner, you could rely on established procedures to guide what you did, and how and when you did it. These procedures served as a checklist to make sure that you accomplished each important step and that the steps were taken in the appropriate order. However, outstanding results are not achieved by following recipes. If that were the case, to become a master chef would require only that you purchase and follow a master chef's recipe book. But, as many cookbooks as celebrity chef Emeril Lagasse may have sold, just reading his books and following his recipes will not make you Lagasse's equal in the kitchen. It takes more.

As noted in the introduction, each step provides a foundation for the next. The procedures and rules learned at the beginner step and the functional skills and strategic decision making learned at the capable level give you the basis for understanding the timing and momentum in thought and action of the competent performer. But where do those timing and momentum skills come from?

Timing and momentum skills come first by understanding your business environment—the people, the resources, and how things work.

A study of exceptional sales professionals revealed that they do not engage the sales process in a linear or procedural fashion.[14] Rather, they move around the sales process in what appears to be an almost random manner, until the researchers looked closer. Salespeople meet clients on an almost infinite number of points along their clients' decision-making processes, and the salespeople are not privy to all the information clients use to make their decisions. Competent salespeople therefore use their ability to distinguish the important from the unimportant to collect information relevant to the sales situation as opportunities present themselves. The process is not random. Valuable information is processed, stored, and then brought to bear *when the time is right* to usher the sales episode to a successful outcome.

Knowing what you are good at and how that can be aligned with the forces that drive your industry is critical to understanding the timing and momentum of your decisions and actions. Consider Michael McCafferty on St. Patrick's Day, 1983. On that day he both filed bankruptcy and began a new business. He slept on a used mattress in a bare apartment, lived on credit card debt, and had no job, no money, and no car. But he did have the knowledge and skills to show fledgling businesses how to solve common and recurring problems with computers.

With no funds for advertising and no car to make sales calls, he needed to make some critical decisions that would attract clients—

and quickly! In his cashless wallet, he found an old clipping listing ten rules for entrepreneurs. He reworked the list into a poster and gave it the title "The 10 Commandments for Managing a Young, Growing Company." McCafferty put his name and phone number at the bottom and smooth-talked a printer into producing two hundred copies on credit.

Next, he enlisted Marianne, an attractive friend of a friend. McCafferty offered to pay her a percentage of the profits from every client she recruited. She delivered the posters to every business in a large industrial park and said only, "Computers? If you would like more information, call the number at the bottom of the poster." Then she walked away. When the phone began to ring, Michael asked the prospective clients what problems they had with their business and offered them computer-based solutions. Because he knew which decisions needed to be made and when, Michael McCafferty had twenty-five clients in a short time, Marianne had $2,000 in commissions, and a new business was born.[15]

It is often most difficult to know what to do and when to do it when few, or apparently no, options are available. In Michael's case there were few standard business models that would have led to success. But Michael knew which decisions to make and when to make them. Timing and momentum in decision making are key factors in becoming a competent businessperson. Unlike Michael, most business professionals operate in an organization. In this setting the timing and momentum aspects of decisions and actions affect other people. You can make a good decision, but if people in your organization are not ready for it, it will be the wrong one.

When your business environment includes a corporate structure, you need to understand not only the external environment in which your clients and customers live but also the internal environment of your organization—its people, resources, structure, and mission. You must be able to read the situation to influence the outcome. Former General Electric CEO Jack Welch put it this way: "What determines your destiny is not the hand you're dealt; it's how you play the hand. And the best way to play your hand is to face reality—see the world the way it is—and act accordingly."[16]

Therefore, it is usually best for you to begin by understanding, first, how decisions and plans are made in your organization and, second, how actions are initiated and measured. Then you need to know how your decisions and actions affect your coworkers. You must understand this from your coworkers' perspective, not yours. Most people will climb on board if they believe your decisions and plans represent a value proposition for them. In other words, if they believe what you are planning on doing will have positive benefits for them, then they will be inclined to align themselves with you. This is as true for your coworkers as it is for your clients. In any situation, therefore, you will gain an advantage by understanding what the others in the room or situation are thinking and what they need. This information will serve you well in timing your decisions and undertaking actions.

The timing of a decision and subsequent actions are as important as the decision itself. All rely on the wisdom that comes from experience in making decisions, knowledge of the critical aspects of your business environment, and skills to undertake the actions subsequent to your decisions in the business world.

Avoiding the Competence Trap

In a typical workplace, the great majority of people are satisfied with being competent. They get the job done and get it done in a timely and reasonably accurate manner. Businesses cannot run without competent people doing what businesses need done. Like a cog in a finely made watch, competent performers can be relied on to do their part time and again. They are appreciated for their dependability, knowledge, and skills. Employers and colleagues become comfortable with those who are competent, and in return competent people become comfortable with consistently meeting the expectations of others. For many people, the majority perhaps, the journey toward becoming expert ends here. But after years of being competent, some people find they have a desire to do better. For personal and professional reasons, they aspire to perform at a higher level. They seek to gain new experiences, increase their knowledge, and hone their skills. They want to know more and do more, and do their job better than they have ever done it before. They search for the next set of challenges.

For those at the competent level, a few learning modalities appear particularly useful for advancing to the next level of expertise. You may find that you are now learning more from others and less from experience. In particular, interactions with both colleagues and competitors are especially instructive. As you are already fairly familiar with your colleagues' thinking, you look increasingly to your competitors for new ideas and innovations. You especially want to know what they are doing right. Additionally, the resources—seminars, training programs, Web sites, books—that you found helpful when you were capable serve you even better as you move to the next level of expertise. You are beginning to get a clearer picture of what you don't know, and these resources can pinpoint the information you seek.

Good coaching and mentoring can significantly accelerate learning, particularly by identifying the knowledge and skills that will elevate your performance and structuring metrics to help you evaluate your progress. Setting goals, devising practice activities, selecting appropriate evaluation standards, and offering constructive feedback are all functions of a good coach. Many competent people find it best to have a coach from outside their immediate work environment. Coaches can bring informed perspectives and fresh information, and they have the skills to take you to the next step along the journey toward becoming expert: proficient. Good coaches will also offer you exercises to improve your overall performance. Complete expertise exercises 11–14 to better reinforce the concepts from this chapter and prepare you for receiving the information on your next step.

Summary

Competent performers

- Use goals and long-term plans to guide decisions and actions
- Distinguish important from unimportant factors when analyzing situations or events
- Plan contingently
- Have a sense of timing and momentum in making decisions and taking actions

GUIDING ACTIONS WITH GOALS AND LONG-TERM PLANS

The actions of competent individuals are guided more by goals and long-term plans than by immediate concerns or situations. Identify below some immediate, intermediate, and long-term goals and some long-term plans that may serve to guide your actions.

Within one week: _____

_____

_____

Within one month: _____

_____

_____

Within six months: _____

_____

_____

Within one year: _____

_____

_____

Within five years: _____

_____

_____

EXPERTISE EXERCISE 12

DISTINGUISHING WHAT'S IMPORTANT IN YOUR BUSINESS WORLD

Recall a recent business experience involving other people. First, identify three important factors you observed in that experience and the information each provided that was useful for taking appropriate action. Next, describe what action you took (or could have taken) based on that information that led (or could have led) to a successful outcome.

Factor 1: _____

    Action: _____

_____

_____

Factor 2: _____

    Action: _____

_____

_____

Factor 3: _____

    Action: _____

_____

_____

PLANNING YOUR OPTIONS

Contingency planning is a tool that competent people use to ensure that they have a healthy complement of options for any activity they intend to undertake. In this exercise make three contingent (if-then) plans: a plan you will complete today, a plan you will complete six months from now, and a plan you will complete in one year.

Today: _____

_____

_____

In six months: _____

_____

_____

In one year: _____

_____

_____

DEVELOPING YOUR CRITICAL SKILLS

List, in descending order, three work-related skills that, if improved, will have the biggest impact on your performance in the next twelve months. For each skill, list two practice activities and a metric you can use to measure your progress in developing the skill.

Critical skill 1: _____

    Practice activity 1: _____

    Practice activity 2: _____

    Progress metric: _____

Critical skill 2: _____

    Practice activity 1: _____

    Practice activity 2: _____

    Progress metric: _____

Critical skill 3: _____

    Practice activity 1: _____

    Practice activity 2: _____

    Progress metric: _____

FIVE

PRACTICING PROFICIENCY

Competent performers do their job well, but those who step up to the proficient level of expertise not only get the job done well, they achieve results that are clearly and consistently above the standard. Proficient people are in the top 25 percent of their field in terms of experience, knowledge, skills, and performance. Few people know more, can do more, or outperform those who are proficient. In fact, only experts consistently outperform the proficient.

In top organizations, a significant number of people are proficient performers. An organization cannot consistently outperform the competition without people whose level of accomplishment is unfailingly above average. Proficient performers work harder and longer than most other people, but what really sets them apart is that they also work smarter and more skillfully. Gaining expertise takes exceeding dedication. Proficient performers dedicate themselves to actively searching for opportunities to gain new knowledge and perspectives, continually practicing and refining requisite skills, and working to learn all they can from their experiences.

Although proficient performers share many of the characteristics of capable and competent performers, they have additional characteristics that contribute to higher performance levels. Proficient performers

- Have a strong sense of personal responsibility
- Have highly developed perceptual skills
- Use efficient routines to handle everyday tasks
- Analyze and solve problems with forward thinking
- Predict future events with a high degree of accuracy

Having a Strong Sense of Personal Responsibility

In 1977, the U.S. steel industry struggled to compete with foreign companies that could produce and ship steel to America cheaper than American companies could produce it. Many executives in the industry begged for government protection from the imports, but not Ken Iverson, CEO at Nucor. Iverson saw the imports as a blessing and spoke out against protectionist government policies. He saw the problems facing American steel as first and foremost stemming from poor management and the fact that management had failed to keep pace with innovation. In Iverson's tenure at Nucor, the stock of the company outperformed the stock market five times over.[1]

If you were to ask me for one characteristic that would differentiate the good from the great in any field, it would be this: feeling responsible. Those who achieve great heights in business, sports, or any other human endeavor do so largely because they believe the outcome is firmly in their hands. They feel that their level of achievement is chiefly their responsibility. Those who achieve less can easily find myriad reasons for a lack of success that reside outside their sphere of influence.

When you feel responsible for your success or lack of it, you work hard to learn whatever is necessary to become successful. When you believe that what you achieve is beyond your control, you give up responsibility for the outcomes of your actions and are therefore less inclined to work to turn a lackluster performance into an outstanding one. Less expert professionals lose sleep worrying about what might happen to them. Proficient performers lose sleep devising ways to be better tomorrow than they were today. They believe their efforts are ultimately measured in results, not in following procedures or completing tasks. For the most part, *how* they accomplish something is secondary to *what* they accomplish.

Proficient performers take control of their destiny by planning their course of action.

Proficient performers hold themselves accountable for problems and deficiencies they encounter, believing that the solutions to these problems reside within their capabilities and responsibilities. When problems arise or an action does not achieve the anticipated result, they analyze the situation, seeking alternatives that might produce the desired result when a similar situation arises.

It is not only those at the elite level of an organization who can take control of their actions. Fred Shea does not have a corner office, keys to a corporate jet, or an administrative assistant. Fred is a postman. He delivers mail. His level of proficiency is so great, however, that he inspired Mark Sanborn, one of the people on Fred's daily route, to write the national best seller *The Fred Factor*. What was the first principle Mark learned from Fred? "Everyone makes a difference. . . . Nobody can prevent you from choosing to be exceptional."[2] You are responsible for the difference you make.

This is a critical component in developing expertise, because when you feel personally responsible, you work diligently to produce a satisfactory—or even superior—outcome. When you believe you have no control over or responsibility for an event, you can more easily walk away from failure, and thus not make the effort to take with you the lessons it may hold for the future. If you don't feel responsible for your mistakes, then you don't do anything about them, and consequently you never improve. Proficient performers take responsibility for their shortcomings, inadequacies, and failures and therefore seize the opportunity to change for the better. The quality of their performance is clearly up to them. They wouldn't have it any other way.

One evening when I was attending a dinner with the editors of *Golf* magazine, the discussion turned to the greatest golf shots ever hit. Carol Mann, a U.S. Open champion and LPGA Hall of Fame member, was at the table, so I asked her, "What was the greatest shot you ever hit in a tournament?" Without hesitation, Carol replied, "My tee shot on 16 in the final round of my U.S. Open win. I pulled it a little left and it stopped just inches from going out of bounds." Jaws dropped. When champions recall their greatest shots, they normally describe shots that flew through two time zones or a putt that tracked across the Andes Mountains before falling over the lip of the last hole—not a shot that stopped just inches from going out of bounds.

In a subsequent e-mail Carol wrote, "I had dreamed about this shot the night before—in my dream the ball went out. That fear was with me all day, and I tried to make some birdies before I got [to 16] so that in case I actually did go out, I would have a cushion of a lead." I gave Carol's comments considerable thought and began to realize how critical her perspective was to her being a champion.

Often we think champions are made in the great shots or great business moves that they execute at critical moments; but champions are also made in the mistakes they minimize or avoid. They take full responsibility for their weaknesses and mistakes, and therefore focus as much attention and energy on eliminating or diminishing them as they do on building and capitalizing on their strengths.

Having Highly Developed Perceptual Skills

Had you been a student at Cornell University in the fall of 1946, you might have witnessed, or perhaps even joined in, a food fight in one of the dining halls. A young professor named Richard was there, and as objects streaked through the air, one spinning plate with the university insignia stamped along the edge piqued his curiosity. As the plate spun through the air, Richard noticed that the wobbling of the edge increased as the spinning of the plate decreased. Most of us would have been more concerned with avoiding those flying plates than with noticing their rate of spin and wobble. This moment was, however, an epiphany for this young professor. As a physicist, he wondered whether the same phenomenon occurred in the electrons of atoms. His thoughts and experiments following that food fight led years later to Professor Richard Feynman being awarded the Nobel Prize for his fundamental work in the field of quantum electrodynamics.[3]

With their considerable accumulated experience and knowledge, proficient performers, like the young professor Feynman, perceive subtleties in the environment that can have profound significance. Years of experience and extensive knowledge have honed their perceptions to the point where anomalies are readily detected. In the business world, having a keen sense of timing comes from an intimate understanding of how one's industry and organization work. With an inability to discern the important from the unimportant, people on the lower steps of expertise struggle to effectively identify, and thus respond to, the most critical situational factors.

Business is a dynamic process where many people with different responsibilities, backgrounds, skills, and interests are engaged in the

myriad activities of an industry. While understanding business ma-
neuverings is essential, being able to focus on the individuals and
events that have the greatest effect on the outcome is critical. Being
able to correctly interpret the significance of unfolding events in business enables proficient performers to recognize the winds of opportunity in a meeting, market, or industry and to adroitly change the
course of action in a direction leading to greater success.

While beginner, capable, and competent performers often see the
symptoms, proficient performers see past the symptoms to identify
the cause of errors or inferior performance. By identifying the cause,
you can provide the appropriate cure more easily.

**A multitude of symptoms can be cured by eliminating the
cause.**

In a study of the professional orientations of the top one hundred
golf instructors in America, many viewed themselves as "repair" people. One instructor stated this important skill this way: "Every mistake
or swing fault has a reason; when you fix a problem at its cause you
can really help someone progress."[4]

Accurate perceptions and insightful interpretations begin with
up-to-date awareness regarding the conditions around you. In other
words, *situational awareness* is an important precursor to performing
well. A study of general-aviation pilots shed some light on this topic.
The pilots who scored better on situational awareness tasks were not
necessarily those with the most flight hours. While all of the pilots
with more than one thousand flight hours had high situational awareness scores, the scores of the remaining pilots, in both the experienced
and beginner groups, were not predicted by flight hours. The researchers concluded that flight hours were not predictive of situational awareness. Rather, pilots with greater skill in aircraft handling,

cockpit task management, task prioritization, and communication coordination, along with greater psychomotor abilities, were more situationally aware.[5] This study suggests that developing skills to levels of automatic performance eases attention demands, enabling people to concentrate less on skill mechanics and more on the situational factors that shape optimum performance. An automatic performance occurs when a skill becomes so highly developed that it takes no conscience thought to perform it—it is automatic. In everyday life, skills such as sitting, standing, walking, and typing are often performed with more thought devoted to the outcome than to the execution of the skill. Automatic skill performance, also known as *automaticity,* is a critical and often-used quality of an expert (discussed in greater detail in chapter 6). It is common, however, for proficient performers to begin to display automaticity in some of their repeatedly used business skills.

Obtaining up-to-date and accurate information in business can prove a challenge for those at the top of the management hierarchy. Seldom do staff want to be the bearers of bad news, especially if they believe such news reflects on their performance. Often information that CEOs receive is polished to take off the negative edge or is kept from them entirely. A recent study found that this was one reason many CEOs held inaccurate perceptions of their organization. In a survey of 124 CEOs and 579 other senior executives around the world, 52 percent of the non-CEOs reported that their teams did poorly in critical areas such as innovative thinking, leading change, developing talent, and building company culture. Only 28 percent of the CEOs reported problems in these areas.[6] Therefore, it is imperative that corporate leaders have firsthand observations and information regarding key elements of their industry. This point was not lost on Sam Walton, who believed that "if we don't have customer satisfaction at the cash register, none of us have a job." He instituted a company policy that required all corporate staff to spend one week each year working as a salesclerk in a Wal-Mart store.[7]

Having highly developed perceptual abilities is not solely the domain of businesspeople. Being able to identify and respond to those things that are both important and within one's control is key to superior performance across the board.

Ivan Lendl was still moving up the ladder to the top of the tennis world when he achieved his first major victory—the 1984 French Open. This event was especially noteworthy because it revealed qualities in his character that would carry him to the ultimate level of expertise. In the final match of that championship, he was down two sets to none to the year's leading player, John McEnroe. Despite the large deficit, the twenty-four-year-old Lendl fought back to win the last three sets and capture his first of eight major championships. It was a feat that is still talked about today.

Being curious, when given the opportunity I asked Lendl what was going through his mind at the time. He said candidly that he wasn't thinking about the score, the match, or even that it was a major championship. He focused completely on each shot before him. He played one stroke at a time, one point at a time. His complete attention was devoted to winning the present point and nothing else. "Before I knew it," he said, "I was ahead and the momentum had shifted. *But I just kept my focus on the next stroke, and let the rest take care of itself.*"

It was deceptively simple. I wanted to say, "That's it?" But I realized the level of focus he was talking about is far deeper than the casual attention most of us give to the tasks before us. During the clamor and turmoil of a major championship, Lendl kept his focus on the essential element of the game of tennis and the one thing he could most control—the shot before him. I've often thought about the lesson behind Ivan's comment:

Recognize the environmental elements most critical for your success and give them your complete attention and your best effort.

Using Efficient Routines
to Handle Everyday Tasks

Established routines help proficient performers minimize time devoted to everyday, mundane, repetitive tasks so they can better manage their time and focus on issues and challenges that require more thought and attention. Routines are common in everyday life, from the time we get out of bed and off to work until we return home and retire at night. Efficient routines form the bedrock of how we orchestrate daily tasks efficiently. Unfortunately, we also tend to develop unproductive routines—gossiping, surfing the Internet, watching television, and so forth. We often waste time simply because something has become routine.

Organizations tend to have routines for handling tasks such as ordering, shipping, invoicing, and processing goods and services when attempting to do business with other organizations. But a 2002 study of 494 firms in the *Journal of International Business Management* reveals that adoption of standardized business routines and an unwillingness to adapt marketing practices seem to be associated with less success when entering new markets.[8] Clearly, routines that improve efficiency in one place or at one time may not work in all situations. When routines detract from success, they need revision to be effective.

Proficient business professionals, however, avoid these empty routines by focusing on getting things done.[9] They have a large toolbox of strategies to accomplish important tasks, and they use these strategies as a matter of routine. For example, when reading a newspaper, they may skim the pages for a solution to a pressing problem or for information that may provide an advantage. When picking up the newspaper, they may say, "So what might be in here today that I can use?"

Analyzing and Solving Problems
with Forward Thinking

Decisions are made in the real, not the theoretical, world. Although many theories exist to guide strategic planning and decision making, professionals often find themselves forced to make complex decisions in unexpected circumstances. A study of the decision making of eighteen primary-care physicians offers an intriguing insight into how proficient performers make decisions.

A researcher worked with each physician to develop a task diagram of the various steps in which the doctor acquired patient information and incorporated it into decision making. The proficient decision makers demonstrated greater flexibility and a more automatic flow in their processes, which freed them to take advantage of new systems and limited their searches and processes to those essential to the situation. Consequently, proficient doctors responded well to unplanned situations and opportunities. Interestingly, the proficient doctors generated an "attentional surplus." Their efficient information retrieval and the automatic nature of certain decisions meant that they required less attention than beginner decision makers, leaving them with additional time to attend to other tasks.[10]

As a proficient performer, when you start to solve a problem you try to better understand the problem by analyzing it qualitatively. You rely on your extensive knowledge to construct a mental representation of the problem, from which you can

- Infer relations to help define the situation

- Identify constraints

- Isolate factors causing the problem and evaluate them

- Justify possible solutions

By analyzing and representing problems in this manner, you rely more on underlying principles and metaphors than on using literal and practical categorizations.

In solving problems, proficient people tend to use forward reasoning, working forward from known facts to the unknown, in contrast with backward reasoning, working backward from a hypothesis or to the known facts.[11] Backward problem solving is characteristic of those who are not yet proficient. Due to knowledge and skill limitations, they have a restricted set of solutions available. Therefore, when a problem arises, less proficient problem solvers usually select a solution they think will work and then reason backward to justify their selection. An old adage applies here: When all you have is a hammer, every problem looks like a nail.

Proficient problem solvers have a greater range of both knowledge and skills, are driven to devise the best solution possible, and are willing to construct an innovative or unique solution, if necessary. As a result, they invest time in carefully collecting all the facts before making decisions.

Proficient problem solvers realize that if they don't get the problem right, there is no hope of getting the solution right.

Proficient problem solvers sometimes may be slower than beginners in the early stages, but overall, they still solve problems faster.[12] More important, the solutions derived by the proficient decision makers using forward reasoning tend not only to produce superior results but also to be more permanent. That is, not only do the solutions lead to better outcomes but they will less likely need to be changed, revised, or replaced.

An interesting study of managerial problem solving in the Netherlands revealed several valuable insights.[13] Some 115 managers were asked to diagnose and solve business cases. Capable and competent managers actually identified more case facts than did proficient managers, primarily because the more expert managers identified only those facts relevant to solving the case. Less expert managers identified both relevant and irrelevant facts. Due to their focusing on only relevant facts and relying on experiential versus theoretical knowledge, the proficient managers solved the cases more accurately and in less time than the capable and competent managers.

One reason that solutions reached by proficient decision makers are both more permanent and more accurate stems from these decision makers' relying more on underlying principles that may be creating the problem than on the surface features of the problem.[14] For example, a beginner manager may see a customer service problem being caused by an employee's particular personality. A proficient manager not only recognizes the individual's uniqueness but also reviews environmental factors that may be causing the problem, and then considers the underlying principles of human interaction and motivation. Essentially this means that the more proficient manager gathers all relevant facts before constructing a solution and then steeps the solution in proven principles rather than immediate concerns. As may be obvious, extensive experience and knowledge are required to develop the skill of proficient decision making.

Herb Kelleher, former president of Southwest Airlines, offers a poignant, if not humorous, point regarding the importance of analyzing problems: "Say there is a problem with anything. I—or somebody—goes out and experiences the problem. Someone says the bin doors don't work. I want to see them not work, to feel them. How can I talk to Boeing about it if I haven't actually had the experience of it malfunctioning? How can I call Boeing and say, 'There's something wrong with the bin doors.' They'd say, 'Oh really, what?' And I'd have to say, 'Well, I don't know. I just heard that they're not working.'"[15]

Accurately Predicting Future Events

We don't really believe proficient or expert performers have a crystal ball, but it often appears as if they do. Because proficient performers are extraordinarily good at recognizing similarities across situations, they can predict, or at least anticipate, potential and likely outcomes of unfolding events with a high degree of accuracy and precision.

A study comparing teachers with little, average, and above-average expertise demonstrated this ability.[16] The researchers asked teachers to view a series of slides of classroom events and comment about what they were thinking. The proficient teachers provided rich commentaries on their observations and drew on their experiences to make judgments about what they saw. They made many assumptions about what they saw, attempted to interpret the meaning of the events, and then inferred relationships between the actions observed and the likely outcomes.

The ability to predict potential outcomes proves useful in selecting activities because only those activities and strategies with the greatest chance of success are selected. For example, consultants' ability to predict which strategies and resources will help their clients improve in the most economical and efficient manner is a major benefit of proficient thinking. Being able to reasonably predict the success of an action plan can save time because you don't need to restart or retry the plan. Being able to predict the level of success increases the likelihood of a quality outcome.

Being able to anticipate and predict likely events is based on years of experience in, and extensive knowledge of, the specific environment.

Having seen similar situations again and again, you can become skilled at anticipating the outcomes of your actions, responses, and behaviors. To accurately predict outcomes, proficient performers review actions, experiment with new ideas, converse with colleagues, and want passionately to find the solution that is in the best interest of the organization.

Research from Australia offers some exciting insights into using video-based perceptual training to improve anticipation skills and decision making.[17] The study used three groups of elite softball players: trained, placebo, and control. In a laboratory setting, the trained group watched various game scenarios on videotape. At the beginning of the session, the players were instructed to focus their attention on particular anticipatory cues and then were asked questions to stimulate cue awareness and anticipatory judgment. Twelve ten-minute training sessions were conducted over four weeks. The researchers discovered that the trained group developed anticipatory and decision-making skills superior to those of the other groups. More important, these skills were shown to transfer to the field environment and live game play.

Anticipatory skills can be learned, and the advantages they offer are well worth the effort for proficient performers. Imagine the advantage you gain when you can accurately anticipate the future.

Taking the Final Step

Few people can achieve the level of performance consistently reached by proficient performers. Being proficient puts you in the top 25 percent of practicing professionals in your business or industry. You are in honored company. You can easily be satisfied with being within this elite circle. There are, however, those for whom being one of the best is not the same as being the best they can be.

For those who measure their performance by what they believe to be their potential and best efforts rather than by the achievements or standards of others, there is never a moment in which they feel they have succeeded completely. If this describes you, then you have an internal urge to move forward and experience new challenges, to learn more about what you do, and to execute your actions to greater effect. You have a passion and a drive that are never satisfied. Moving to the next step, expert, is not usually a conscious choice. Rather, moving to this step is more an attempt to satisfy a need to know, a belief that you can be better, and the knowledge that the only real limits placed on you are those you place yourself.

While proficient performers assume significant responsibility for personal and professional progress, notice similarities across situations, use well-established routines for everyday tasks, have heightened perceptual capacities, and show a greater sophistication in analyzing problems and deriving solutions, they still remain largely analytic and deliberate in their decision making as well as routine in their actions. That is, they still demonstrate a logical progression in their decision making and rely on patterned practices to carry out their daily tasks. But these are not necessarily the ways of experts or the top professional performers.

Several types of learning may help propel proficient performers to the final step of expertise. First, your interactions with others, both in your field and out, help you gain new perspectives on old problems, discover innovative strategies that work, and provide fresh leads to more knowledge. Working with people in your field keeps you apprised of trends and changes. Working with people outside your field can help you bring innovative ideas to bear on old problems. Having learned much from their own experiences, proficient performers look to sources outside themselves for fresh ideas and innovations for knowledge critical to planning and decision making.

Peers, clients, and resources such as conferences, books, and videotapes become important sources of information to increase knowledge, but proficient performers find these sources a great reservoir of new skills that can be applied to their business. By tapping sources completely outside your field or profession, you can witness and practice skills from many areas, which can provide new revelations for your industry or profession. Many in business, for example, find communication skills effective for motivating employees, presenting plans to supervisors or board members, and interacting with clients. Because increased skill in communication is likely to improve the performance of any business professional, outside sources offer potent learning sources for guidance, models, and instruction. As described in the next chapter, the best performers never stop learning. If you are ready to learn what it takes to reach the final step in becoming expert, complete expertise exercises 15–18 and then turn the page to go forward!

Summary

Proficient performers

- Have a strong sense of personal responsibility
- Have highly developed perceptual skills
- Use efficient routines to handle everyday tasks
- Analyze and solve problems with forward thinking
- Predict future events with a high degree of accuracy

EXPERTISE EXERCISE 15

TAKING RESPONSIBILITY

Identify a recent experience where the outcome was not to your liking. How much of that outcome was under your control? What will you do differently if a similar situation arises?

_____

_____

_____

_____

_____

EXPERTISE EXERCISE 16

PERFORMING ROUTINE TASKS

Identify a task or a series of tasks you routinely perform in the course of your professional duties and describe them briefly.

The purpose or outcome of the task(s): _____

_____

How you regularly perform the task(s): _____

_____

How the task(s) can be performed more efficiently: _____

_____

_____

How much time you would gain each time you performed the task(s) more efficiently: _____

MAKING DECISIONS THAT MAKE A DIFFERENCE

Identify a problem you are currently facing and complete the steps below.

Clearly define the problem: _____

_____

_____

Isolate the factors (not the symptoms) causing the problem: _____

_____

_____

_____

Identify the constraints in finding solutions: _____

_____

_____

_____

_____

Evaluate possible solutions in terms of time, cost, and the likelihood of permanently solving the problem: _____

_____

_____

_____

_____

HARNESSING OUTSIDE RESOURCES

List three fields that can serve as effective information resources for your industry (e.g., psychology, sociology, engineering). For each field identify one specific resource you might use to gain knowledge, skills, or innovative insights (e.g., a book, consultant, or seminar).

Field 1: _____

    Resource: _____

Field 2: _____

    Resource: _____

Field 3: _____

    Resource: _____

SIX

EXCELLING TO EXPERT

Experts are individuals who consistently outperform their peers—no one does it better than an expert. A group of experts may have different experiences, embrace different knowledge, use different skills, but they all consistently produce superior results. To state the obvious, experts have more experience, knowledge, skills, and success in their field than almost anyone. They are the best at what they do, and their record of performance proves it. This does not mean that experts can necessarily outperform everyone every time in every circumstance; rather, on an overall, long-term basis, expert performers get more done in less time, in more places, and with superior results more often than less expert performers do.

Interestingly, few experts see themselves as expert. Most see themselves as works in progress, that is, as still needing greater knowledge and increased skills, and still able to learn a great deal more from their experiences. Perhaps this perspective explains how they became experts in the first place.

Experts are all too aware that if they don't continue to make the effort to learn from experience, gain more knowledge, and develop new skills, they will be quickly surpassed by those who do. Therefore, experts are among the greatest learners in their respective fields. First and foremost, they read. The written word remains the most prominent source of knowledge in advanced civilizations. A true expert does not overlook such important sources of information. Experts also have highly developed networks of relationships. But it was not who they know that got them to the top; it was listening to the people they know that got them there. Experts use networks as a source of new insights, information, and skills—not for self-promotion.

The skills of experts are their signatures. To watch experts at work is to watch those who perform with what appears to be ease but certainly defines fluidity, gracefulness, and precision. Their professional skill sets are as extensive as they are refined; and, in an effort to constantly improve their performance, experts work continuously to sharpen their skills. Experts are also creative innovators. If a solution to a problem does not exist, or the present solutions are lacking, experts will devise or discover new methods, techniques, processes, or positions to elevate their personal and professional performance. The level of performance experts achieve is linked directly to the characteristics that define their presence in the workplace. Experts

- Seek knowledge insatiably
- Have a superior memory
- Attend to the atypical
- Plan extensively and act intuitively
- Execute skills gracefully and automatically
- Meet inadequacies and failures with corrective action
- Are self-monitoring

Seeking Knowledge Insatiably

While it is obvious that experts have extensive knowledge, the importance of this characteristic demands that it be examined thoroughly. Business professionals who make the final step and become experts have made, and continue to make, significant investments in learning all they can about their industry, the requisite skills for good performance, and every factor that may influence the final outcome of their efforts. People seek more knowledge for a long list of reasons, but for experts that list inevitably includes passion for what they do. Meeting experts, you find people who enjoy talking endlessly about their business, seek others' views on pertinent topics, and have extensive libraries devoted to subjects that affect their enterprise.

Experts use extensive resources to build large stores of knowledge. Experience and colleagues represent essential sources of knowledge, but books, journals, and magazines, as well as conferences, education programs, and clients are also important sources for experts' knowledge.[1] Legendary IBM leader Thomas J. Watson Sr. was a knowledge sponge and offered insight into an important skill required of those seeking to scale the summit of the business world:

> Listening is one of the best ways in the world to learn. Sometimes we don't take the time to listen to the other fellow. That sometimes applies to the man when he is a supervisor. His manager is trying to tell him something, but he doesn't listen, he doesn't have his mind open. Sometimes you reverse that. Sometimes the man up above does not take the time to listen to other men, the men below him. Then he often loses a whole lot of knowledge and misses one of the greatest opportunities to study. We must therefore listen to each other.[2]

As you move up executive levels, you move further away from where the action takes place. It is easy to lose touch with what is really going on in the organization. A study of more than two hundred thousand executives, managers, and business professionals found that the most successful executives use a leadership style that keeps the information pipeline open and the critical data flowing freely.[3] The open pipeline, in turn, feeds the evolving thinking style of the analytic, information-hungry senior executive focused on finding the right answer. This skill manifests in public when senior executives encourage employees to offer information. In private, they use that information to narrow down options and identify the best one.

Taking this one step further, Stephen Covey describes highly effective people as those who "seek first to understand, then be understood." Specifically, he explained that empathetic listeners are those who "get inside another person's frame of reference. You look out through it, you see the world the way they see the world, you understand their paradigm, you understand how they feel."[4] Empathetic listening is "so powerful because it gives you accurate data to work with. Instead of projecting your own autobiography and assuming thoughts, feelings, motives, and interpretation, you're dealing with reality inside another person's head and heart."[5] The depth and accuracy of that data is a valued source of knowledge for experts.

People who aspire to be the best they can be at what they do are sponges, constantly absorbing fresh ideas and information.

To stop learning is to never improve. Experts know that. Lower-level performers are generally satisfied with what they know and, surprisingly, believe they pretty much know all they need to know.[6] This point was particularly well illustrated by Florida State University coach Bobby Bowden as quoted earlier: "When I stop learning and adjusting, nobody will have to tell me to retire."[7]

Expert performers' superior knowledge permits them to use the workplace environment to great effect. For example, they demonstrate greater flexibility in using equipment or technology for greater efficiency of operation than lower-level performers. Make no mistake, however; experts do not use the latest and greatest technology only because it is available or because everyone else is using it. Only if a new piece of equipment will help them complete tasks with greater efficiency and produce greater quality will they consider using it.[8]

Experts do not collect information simply as a matter of habit or interest. They can tap their extensive knowledge to envision many ways of using equipment, skills, strategies, facts, facilities, or objects for multiple purposes, whereas those with less expertise might perceive only a single purpose.

Never one to waste anything for which a good purpose could be found, Dr. Waldo Semon, a leading chemist for the B.F. Goodrich Company, was using a chunk of industrial by-product as a paperweight. One morning in 1926, as he sat behind his desk, he pondered the paperweight. He thought to himself that, if he could find a way to make the substance pliable, perhaps it could be shaped into something useful. He thought some more and soon worked out a way to make his paperweight supple enough to pass through an extruder, a machine that shapes manufactured products. What was at one time only Dr. Semon's paperweight is now known to the world as polyvinyl chloride, or PVC, and people continue to find virtually countless uses for it to this day.

Interestingly, when experts are faced with relevant topics with which they have little or no familiarity, they take measures to gain understanding. They take pains to talk with people who are experts on the topic, read pertinent materials, and even work on developing their own mastery of required skills. When you recognize the importance of your personal understanding of a subject in bringing it to bear on your success, you are seeing the world of information like an expert.

Having a Superior Memory

It would be an exercise in futility if the knowledge you fought so hard to collect and construct filtered out of your memory like sand through a sieve. How are experts able to retain the knowledge they've been able to accumulate? It's not that they are any more intelligent than the average person, necessarily. Rather than large intellectual powers and capacities, they have skills that help them remember what they learn.

Testing the now famous memorist Rajan Mahadevan in a laboratory proved that he can recall from memory a remarkable number of numerals and letters. In 1981, Rajan recalled 31,811 digits of π without an error. In replicating this research, researchers have now come to the conclusion that what originally appeared to be Rajan's innate ability has less to do with his superior memory than his thousand hours of practice in memorizing the mathematical constant π.[9] Rajan learned encoding techniques that helped him memorize large sets of numbers or letters through practice. Memory therefore is more accurately defined as a skill that can be learned rather than a characteristic possessed from birth.

Mark Cuban, founder of MicroSolutions and owner of the professional basketball team the Dallas Mavericks, wrote the following in his blog on May 7, 2004:

It's crazy the things that you remember. . . . I remember reading the PC DOS manual (I really did), and being proud that I could figure out how to set up startup menus for my customers. I remember going to every single retail store in town, BusinessLand, NYNEX, ComputerLand, CompuShop . . . and introducing myself to every salesperson to try to get leads. I would call every single big computer company that did anything at all with small businesses, IBM, Wang, Dec, Xerox, Data General, DataPoint (remember them?), setting meetings, asking to come to their offices since I couldn't afford to take them to lunch. I didn't need a lot of customers, but my business grew and grew. Not too fast, but fast enough that by the time MicroSolutions had been in business about 2 years, I had 85k dollars in the bank.[10]

I would disagree with Mr. Cuban on only one point: It is not crazy the things you remember—it is critical. That Mark Cuban never forgot what brought him success in the computer industry means he remembers the lessons learned and earned in his experiences. He actually noted this crucial point in his blog on April 25, 2004: "It's always the little decisions that have the biggest impact."[11] Experts remember the factors that have the biggest impact because those are the important things to remember.

I discovered another example of an expert's memory while studying the analytical skills of Charlie Sorrell, the 1990 National PGA Teacher of the Year. As part of the study, I had videotaped three golfers. One was an expert player. I asked Charlie to watch the tapes and just tell me what he observed. When we reached the expert player, Charlie exclaimed, "I know her! She took a lesson from me about ten years ago." I had to ask, "How do you know?" He replied, "You see her follow-through? See how she holds the club up? She did that ten years ago. Except it doesn't quite look the same. I wonder if she has a back injury." The player was Kelly Hester, and I asked her if she ever had taken a lesson from Charlie. "Yeah," she replied, "But just one." Then

I asked, "Kelly, do you have back problems?" "Yeah," she replied, "I injured my back about six months ago."

As demonstrated by Rajan, Mark, and Charlie, the memory of an expert is a remarkable attribute. The research of Anders Ericsson and colleagues[12] demonstrates that

Superior memory comes from the ability to encode information as it is stored.

A more recent study not only supports this finding but also offers additional insights that may prove useful for people attempting to improve their memory. In a study of experts' recall memory, two things happened when they encountered new information.[13] First, the experts evaluated the quality of the information. During this process they considered the reliability of the source, the contribution of the information to their current knowledge, and the significance of the information in terms of practical application. As they had since they were at the competent level, these experts sorted the important information from the unimportant in what they observed.

Second, the experts made predictions based on what they thought would happen next. From there they speculated on how they could use this information and on what effect it would have in influencing the next series of events. In short, a key to the superior memory of an expert is found in two questions—the same two questions you can ask yourself the next time you encounter new information regarding your business:

- How good is this information?
- How can I use this information?

If experts are dependent on their memory, will their expertise decline with age-related memory loss? UCLA professor Alan Casel addressed this question. Participants in his research studied sentences that contained numeric quantity, object, and location information (for example, 26 cherries in a bowl). They were later cued with the location and asked to recall the object and its quantity. In general, there were significant age differences for recall of quantity and recall of arbitrary information but negligible age differences for recall of related objects. Interestingly, a group of older retired accountants and bookkeepers showed exceptional memory for numerical information. The findings suggest that experts retain their superior memory for domain-specific information even as they age.[14]

Attending to the Atypical

In 1976, a young economics professor from Chittagong University in Bangladesh lent $27 out of his own pocket to a group of poor craftsmen. To boost the impact of that small sum, Muhammad Yunus volunteered to serve as guarantor on a larger loan from a traditional bank. A strange thing happened that no one in the traditional bank anticipated: The borrowers made good on their loan. This experience kindled the idea for a village-based enterprise called the Grameen Project. The project (and later a bank) was founded on Yunus' conviction that poor people can be both reliable borrowers and avid entrepreneurs—a conviction that ran entirely contrary to the thinking of traditional banks.

But Yunus understood economics and the people of Bangladesh. Therein was the basis for his seeing what was not typical in the banking business. For example, he focused his lending on women because they are most likely to think of family needs. This was a radical step in a traditional Muslim society, but as of this writing, 96 percent of Grameen's borrowers are women. Traditional banks favor large loans to big companies. Grameen offers poor entrepreneurs the small loans they need. Grameen's rate of default is the envy of many larger banks. So astounding were the success and changes that took place with this project that Muhammad Yunus and Grameen Bank were awarded the Nobel Prize in 2005 "for their efforts to create economic and social development from below."[15]

When observing the events of business, experts such as Muhammed Yunus attend to the *atypical* in a situation. When situations are assessed as typical or predictable, experts let events unfold without interference and monitor them with an almost casual attention. On the other hand,

When a situation appears to be unusual, experts attempt to make sense of the anomalies, looking for opportunities or dangers and anticipating outcomes.

Expert business performers closely monitor situations in the business environment. When something atypical occurs, it receives rapid and thorough attention, followed by action. In a classic example, if you were a pharmacist in Chicago in the early 1900s, you might have noticed that several of your competitors began installing a small fountain behind their counter to dispense soda water as a health aid to their customers. Some of the pharmacists would even add a little flavor such as lemon or cherry to improve the otherwise slightly bitter taste of the bubbly water. To Charles Walgreen, this was not a typical activity for a pharmacy, and in it he saw opportunity. When the shop adjacent to his pharmacy became available, he expanded. The expansion featured a large soda fountain with an extended counter for his customers so they could sit comfortably while enjoying their drinks. He also extended the menu by offering sodas with ice cream and ice cream sundaes. Later he added soups and sandwiches to the menu to attract more customers. In attending to the atypical, Charles Walgreen found opportunity.[16]

When things are working in a normal pattern, however, experts tend not to reflect on what is occurring, but rather only monitor the process until something seems out of the ordinary. This conserves energy and does not allow experts to get bogged down in the mundane aspects of the operation. The bigger picture, which is framed by their goals and intentions, remains clearly visible.

It is the everyday anomalies that offer the early signals of both crisis and opportunity. Sometimes they are one in the same. By attending to the atypical, experts are able to see and seize opportunity or avoid disasters long before others and thus gain a decided advantage. When attending to the atypical, experts draw on their extensive and highly organized knowledge to efficiently and economically sift the information to determine their next set of actions.

Planning Extensively and Acting Intuitively

At the competent step in developing expertise, preparation for action became more sophisticated as you planned contingently. As a proficient performer, you devoted more time to analyzing a problem and using pertinent information to think forward toward a workable solution. Experts build on these skills by improving planning and preparation and thereby set themselves up for taking effective, situational actions through intuitive responses.

Extensive Planning

Expert performers have a high regard for planning and being prepared. Despite years of experience, they still feel the need to devise detailed plans to ensure that they meet their desired objectives. One example is former University of North Carolina coach Dean Smith, college basketball's winningest coach. In his 1999 memoir, Coach

Smith explained his view on planning: "Practice was the foundation of everything we did. Our practices were tough, carefully planned, and meticulously organized. . . . Each day, players received a typed copy of our practice plan. They would come into the locker room, and while dressing they would leaf through the plan, which would give them a precise schedule of what we would be working on that day."[17]

Experts see planning as an integral and necessary part of their duties. Basketball coaching great John Wooden dedicated two hours every morning to planning the afternoon's practice. He made notes on index cards and carried them to practice.[18] As he adjusted the plan, he noted the changes on the cards. Later, the schedule and notes were transferred to a notebook for future reference.

The depth of planning increases with one's expertise.[19]

When you are an expert, your planning includes extensive evaluation of available information. You weigh action strategies to determine which external factors are most likely to influence outcomes and which action strategies may prove most effective in navigating the situation to meet the goal or achieve the desired result, given the resources available and the factors likely to be encountered. In preparing for a situation, you carefully review potential strategies relied on in the past and, because you have familiarized yourself with the situation you are about to face, you conceive new actions, which may be better than those used previously. Experts mentally plan out consequences of sequences of actions so they know the cost and benefits of each potential action prior to engagement.[20]

When you are an expert, your planning includes familiarizing yourself thoroughly with many of the factors you will likely face. You organize the knowledge and resources that are most useful in negotiating the events that are likely to occur and assemble a catalog of strategies you can bring to bear on the situation as events unfold. Experts are seldom, if ever, caught unprepared. Experts' planning does not, however, create scripts that they follow to the letter once the situation or event begins. For experts, plans play an important preparatory role, particularly in dynamic and uncertain environments, but they do not inflexibly establish the expert's sequence of actions.[21] The following section explains why.

Intuitive Action

It was a firmly entrenched belief in the pharmaceutical industry that you could not acquire a Japanese company and be profitable. After all, business is done differently there, making it difficult for westerners to understand and navigate the marketplace. But Franz Humer, chairman and CEO of the Roche pharmaceutical firm in Basel, Switzerland, saw opportunity—but he also had something else.[22] Roche already had a seventy-five-year presence in Japan under its own brand name, which helped Humer recognize the tremendous size of the pharmaceutical market there. As part of a deal with Chugai Pharmaceutical Company, Roche would give up its brand and integrate its operations, management, and products into those of the Japanese company. During negotiations, Humer's intuition told him that he could trust his Japanese counterpart across the table. That trust was built on a relationship that had been developed over a five-year period of discussions that had broken off but later resumed. When it came to decision time, Humer went with his gut feeling and closed the deal, and today Chugai Pharmaceutical is one of the top three companies in the world's second-largest pharmaceutical market.

A major divide between expert and less expert is the use of intuition in decision making.

Experts use intuition—shaped by years of experience and sharpened by extensive knowledge—to make many of their most important decisions.

Experts get a gut feeling and have the confidence to go with those feelings—even if those feelings run counter to accepted logic or convention. They know they cannot know everything possible about the situation or the players involved, but they have planned and prepared extensively and are highly attuned to the important events as they unfold. Something has to be the trigger that signals the green or red light, and most often that trigger is the expert's intuitive feeling.

Intuitive decision making is a dangerous practice for beginners, and perhaps for even capable or competent performers, but it is the modus operandi for experts. Years of reflective practice, experimentation, trying, failing, and succeeding are required to gain an expert's intuitive ability. The criterion that separates the expert from the less expert is not the amount of intuition used but rather the superior performances and solutions the process yields.

How do experts develop intuition? According to Humer, "It's a matter of becoming hyperaware of your environment and learning to sense the vibe in the room. Especially in a negotiation setting, I try to have my entire body, my entire mind, all my emotions switched on to 'receiving.' How are people reacting? How are they behaving? If you can enter this mode, you can be sensitive to small changes that other people wouldn't even notice."[23] The genesis of intuition resides in two factors:

- Extensive knowledge
- Extensive familiarity with the environment—that is, experience

The years of study, the assembly of knowledge, and the careful planning are all needed to incubate intuition.

As Humer indicated, it also takes an intimate knowledge of your surroundings. You must know well the players and the activities that make up the social dance of your business. Who will do what, where, when, how, and why? Combined, there is no way to know precisely all of that information. But years of experience in similar business settings percolate with accumulated knowledge to enable you, the expert, to gain a sense of what is likely to happen, where and when it will happen, how, and why—and that sense, that deep feeling in your gut, is intuition. Often, as was the case with Humer in Japan, that feeling can run counter to conventional wisdom.

To develop a deeper intuitive sense for business decisions, you must practice using your intuition when it comes to you—and with experience and knowledge it will develop more. Learn to listen to it and trust it. For many who are schooled in logical analysis, trusting it is the hard part. In the initial phases of practicing intuition, look for a relative low-risk decision and go with the gut feeling when it comes. Soon you will come to trust that feeling like an old friend, and you will find yourself making superior decisions—but with no way to explain them other than "I just had this feeling." Intuition, remember, is not a logical or analytic process; it is indispensable in the decision-making process of experts. Extensive planning and intuitive action are a powerful combination in an expert's arsenal.

Executing Skills Gracefully and Automatically

Gracefully executed skills are a hallmark of experts. The actions of experts account for their outstanding results. Knowledge helps you decide what to do, and your experience helps you know when to do it, but it is *what* you do (that is, the skills you execute) that is directly linked to your performance. In the case of experts, nobody does it better. Experts have a wealth of skills and can perform them nearly flawlessly at the right time in almost any circumstance.

The years of experience and repeated routines in an expert's workday are performed with seemingly little effort, but the results are consistently extraordinary. Expert executives, for example, are highly skilled at planning, executing, and evaluating successful meetings due, in part, to the automatic routines used in conducting the meeting. The meeting may open with a statement of purpose, identification of the modes of interaction, and a closing statement that includes a follow-up. The meeting thus comes off with the optimum results in the least amount of time, largely due to the skillful behavior of the person in charge.

Performing a skill without conscious thought gives the actions of an expert a fluid, graceful, relaxed—almost effortless—appearance. A high degree of automatic behavior, described as experts' *knowing in action*,[24] is characteristic of expert performance. This skilled, automatic behavior is best viewed in an expert's daily routines. These routines are the repetitive activities that seemingly occur with little planning, practice, or forethought.

An expert's automatic behavior stems from the ability to discriminate information early and respond quickly with practiced routines.[25]

For example, a manager may know an employee so well that he detects apprehension while in the midst of an explanation of a new procedure and without much thought offers the employee reassurance that mollifies the apprehension.

This automatic behavior can be a double-edged sword. On one hand, it allows for the relaxed, fluid, unconscious performance of a skill. On the other hand, once a skill becomes automatic, the tendency is to let it lie and never improve it. A case in point: Very few people practice improving everyday communication skills, such as writing or speaking—skills that, if improved, would no doubt improve virtually any business transaction.

It is also important to remember that as you gain experience in business, your web of responsibilities, and the skills necessary to meet those responsibilities, change. Put another way, as the inevitable change in business occurs, new skills are needed. Consider the outstanding performers in an organization who receive a promotion to the C-suite. While the skills they possessed in their previous positions may have made them stars, those skills may not be the same skills they now need to achieve outstanding results. It is common, for example, for those who receive a managerial promotion to be weaned away from individual performance skills in favor of skills that promote team and group performance.[26] The skills that get you promoted are not necessarily the ones that will keep you performing at an expert level. Given the shifting demands and dynamic challenges of business and industry, the development of business skills is an ongoing quest. Those who don't see it that way often wake up one morning wondering how the world has passed them by.

Experts, in their continual quest for improved performance, do not accept their present level of skills simply because it is automatic or comfortable, or because it accounts for their current success. If it will improve their performance, they will improve those skills. Tiger Woods, arguably the greatest golfer in the history of the sport, regularly visits his teacher for lessons. Woods knows that if he wants to improve, he needs a deeper understanding of the skills that lead to that improvement. After that knowledge is acquired, it must be practiced to be ingrained. It is no different in business than in sport.

When we observe the easy, graceful flow of an expert's skill, we often come to the conclusion that the expert is a "natural." No. No one is born an expert, and no one is born skillful. Everyone must learn every skill they possess. While some may learn faster or to a greater level of proficiency, everyone learns skills the same way, and there are few shortcuts. The graceful, fluid performance of an expert is the result, not of any innate quality, but of years of practice. You must work hard at it to be good at it.

Meeting Inadequacies and Failures
with Corrective Action

When asked, "What is Nomura's greatest weakness?" Yoshihisa Tabuchi, CEO of Nomura, the world's largest and most profitable financial institution, replied,

> We haven't had a failure. To me that is a weakness. I think Nomura needs a failure. Past success can be as much a trap as a guide. Markets today are very volatile; the world can change in a day. But some people at Nomura believe that the way we succeeded in the past is the way to succeed in the future. It's natural to want to believe that. But unless you tear yourself away from that kind of thinking, you cripple your ability to cope with change and, more importantly, to create change.[27]

It may seem odd that an industry leader points to the lack of failure as a weakness. But this is not news to experts. To experts, today's failure may hold the key to tomorrow's success. Often the difference between proficient and expert performers is how they handle failure. Those who fear failure are seldom those who excel. Those who learn from their failures are the better for having failed. Experts view failure as an opportunity to learn.[28] Success reveals what you do well. Failure shows you what you can do better. Experts like Mr. Tabuchi are focused on being better. Research supports the notion that the inevitable failures resulting from years of practice and experience are essential to developing expert skill levels.[29] So how do experts make failure work for them? Two processes come into play here. First, experts rigorously analyze the causes of failure. Second, they take corrective action.

Analyzing the Causes of Failure

Because experts see failure as both a natural by-product of attempting to extend current performance levels and an opportunity to learn, they thoroughly analyze the cause of their failures to learn all they can from these experiences. Experts recognize that, in analyzing failure, they can learn to identify and correct deficient practices, reset goals, understand their current limitations, overcome weaknesses, and see possibilities for future performance.[30]

> **The only way to gain advantage from a failure is through a careful, objective, and honest analysis of the causes.**

Without understanding the cause of a failure, correcting the problem or ultimately finding a successful solution is impossible.

A situation does not have to result in a debacle or an obvious flop to receive scrutiny from an expert. For the beginner, capable, or even competent performer, solving the problem meets the goal or expectation. To these professionals, if the problem is solved, it needs no further consideration or thought because it is time to move on to the next challenge or problem. The adequacy or permanency of the solution is not an issue because the problem is solved. Experts think differently.

Although a solution may solve a problem, it may not satisfy the expert who is constantly asking the question "Could I have done that better?" When you ask yourself that question, you are thinking like an expert. You may discover that there is nothing wrong with your solution, decision, or action, but you may also find there may have been a better way. In assessing the quality of their solutions, experts are not looking to judge whether they were right or wrong. Rather, they are looking for a better way. Nothing is wrong with walking as a means of transportation. However, the person who first climbed on a horse found a better way. Nothing was wrong with horses for transportation, but the first person to assemble an automobile found a better way, and so it goes throughout history. In short, experts are rigorous in analyzing the causes of failure or determining the adequacy of the solutions so they can figure out precisely how to achieve success. After they have the root causes and deficiencies in hand, they are ready for the next step: taking corrective action.

Taking Corrective Action

At one time Pioneer Hi-Bred International's sales representatives used handheld terminals to manage their daily sales information. Because they used so many of them, Pioneer bought Norand, the company that made them. Within a few years, laptop computer technology made handheld terminals obsolete. Pioneer sold the terminal company at a significant loss.

Pioneer's practice was to divide a percent of the annual profits equally among employees. In the year of that unprofitable sale, profit-sharing checks were noticeably smaller, and the employees' Pioneer stock values dropped. Soon after, when Pioneer CEO Tom Urban met with the Pioneer employees, he faced a disgruntled group. One employee described Urban's visit this way:

> When he walked into the meeting room for his first visit after the sale of Norand, he acknowledged the group, removed his jacket, and neatly folded it across the back of the chair. He loosened his tie, undid his collar, and rolled up his sleeves. The next thing he said was the last thing I ever expected to hear a CEO say. He said, "I made a mistake buying Norand and I am sorry. I am sorry your

profit-sharing was lower because of the purchase, and I am sorry your stock was hurt by the purchase. I will continue to take risks, but I am a bit smarter now, and I will work harder for you." . . . As I sat listening to him, I knew I could trust him, and that he deserved every bit of loyalty I could give to him and to Pioneer. I recall thinking that I would follow him into any battle.[31]

Tom Urban understood that a mistake had been made, and he assessed both the causes and consequences of that failure. He then took corrective action. In this particular case, Pioneer's employees had been hurt by his actions. Consequently, he took action by recognizing and apologizing for the mistake and by assuring them that their concerns were his concerns. Why did an employee say that Urban's words were "the last thing I ever expected to hear a CEO say"? Because few people will admit mistakes or subsequently take corrective action. Experts do, but perhaps that is one reason we see so few of them: *It takes uncommon courage.*

Failure and rejection. Everyone experiences them. Some succumb. Those who will become expert learn from them. Consider the following examples:[32]

- Lucille Ball was told to forget about acting by her first coach.

- Decca Records informed The Beatles that "groups of guitars are on their way out."

- Dr. Seuss had his first book rejected twenty-seven times before finding a publisher.

- Elvis Presley was told to go back to driving a truck after his first (and only) Grand Ole Opry performance.

- The city leaders of Burbank, California, rejected the idea of a theme park that was submitted by a cartoonist named Walt Disney.

- Michael Jordan was cut from his high school basketball team.

Like us all, each of these people faced failure, but they used it as an opportunity to learn. They learned how to get better and how to succeed. Experts analyze the causes of failure and then take corrective action.

Self-Monitoring

More than one expert has told me, "Just because I know more than most people about this business doesn't mean I know everything there is to know." An interesting phenomenon occurs in almost every field or business. Beginners believe they know a great deal more about the business than do experts. If you ask beginners how much they know in relation to all there is to know about their business, they are likely to tell you about 70 to 80 percent.

Experts are likely to tell you that they know only about 50 to 60 percent of all there is to know about their business.[33]

Obviously it is the expert who knows more, so why the difference in perception?

In reality, when you reach the expert level, you are far better at understanding the limits of your knowledge and skills. You are also more self-critical of your work and love what you do to such a degree that you strive to be even better than you are now—regardless of any success or awards you may have enjoyed. Beginners, in contrast, don't know enough to know just how little they know.

Self-monitoring is the careful observation and tracking of your performance and outcomes.[34] More than mere reflection on your experiences, self-monitoring pushes you to move beyond evaluating your business experiences and engage in critical self-analysis.[35] That's not to say that to be expert you must turn negative and self-deprecating. Rather, you learn to identify elements of your professional practice that merit increased attention and scrutiny.

Goal setting and behavior modification become linked to your ongoing critique of your business performance, and you regularly monitor your progress toward reaching targeted objectives. Self-monitoring serves a wholly intrapersonal and goal-directed process of behavior analysis, modification, and implementation.[36] You become the steward of your professional growth and improvement.

Self-monitoring is not a practice confined to business professionals. It has been traced to superior performances in acting, academic achievement, and sport.[37] Expert physicists, writers, athletes, teachers, and musicians have all used self-monitoring to continue to improve their performance.[38]

As a result of this practice, experts are more aware of errors made and are better at accurately predicting which problems will be most difficult during problem solving.[39] Also, they are superior at understanding why they fail to comprehend certain elements of a problem and are more aware of the appropriateness or adequacy of the solutions they promote. They objectively and honestly assess and identify their shortcomings and knowledge deficiencies with a high degree of precision, making them better able to accurately analyze the causes of their failures and take corrective actions.

Recently, I studied just how experts keep on learning and why it takes people with less expertise longer to understand something.[40] I found that experts in my study closely and extensively monitored the things they do well and the things they believe they can do better. That is, they were keenly aware of the knowledge and skills critical to a good performance and routinely and consciously evaluated the quality of the results they obtained. This self-monitoring led them to identify both goals and actions that led to improved performance. In other words, in reflecting on their experiences and evaluating their performance, experts develop self-improvement plans and programs.

While beginning performers may simply be unaware of how little they know, expert businesspeople are keenly aware of what they still don't know. They also understand why they fail to comprehend certain elements of problems when things don't work as intended. Further, they are acutely aware of the appropriateness or inadequacies of the solutions they attempt and practices they employ.

The founder of Wal-Mart, Sam Walton, revealed signs of self-monitoring, and it showed in his ability to improve his company's performance. When he realized that Wal-Mart had serious purchasing and merchandizing problems in the formative years of the business, he and his store managers critiqued themselves. "When somebody made a bad mistake—whether it was myself or anybody else—we talked about it, admitted it, tried to figure out how to correct it, and then moved on to the next day's work."[41]

Maintaining Expertise

The hallmark of expert business professionals is their consistent and superior performance. They do not necessarily reveal signs of being any more intelligent than anyone else, nor do they necessarily appear to be devoting more effort than others during their performance. (At times they even seem surprisingly relaxed.) But appearances can be deceiving. The skills of experts are extensive, complex, earned over years of experience and deliberate practice, and dependent on extensive knowledge of all facets that affect the outcomes of their performance.

With clear goals, sustained practice, and a thirst for learning and experience, you can move into the elite ranks of your business, trade, or profession. The level of expertise you achieve is yours to determine.

The next chapter, "Navigating the Journey," can help you go as far as you choose to go. But first, complete expertise exercises 19–21. They will help you sustain your journey toward becoming expert.

Summary

Expert performers consistently achieve outstanding results because they

- Seek knowledge insatiably
- Have a superior memory
- Attend to the atypical
- Plan extensively and act intuitively
- Execute skills gracefully and automatically
- Meet inadequacies and failures with corrective action
- Are self-monitoring

SELF-MONITORING

Briefly describe a recent important business experience or event and then answer the questions that follow.

_____

_____

_____

_____

_____

In considering your role in this experience or event, what did you do well?

_____

_____

What could you have done better?_____

_____

_____

How could you have done it better?_____

_____

_____

What can you do to be better prepared should a similar experience occur again?

_____

_____

_____

NETWORKING

List the names of six people you know who possess extraordinary knowledge or skills that may help you perform your job with greater expertise. Then identify a method for communicating with each person to access his or her information. You may want to offer to reverse the process to help that person.

Name 1: _____

    Knowledge/skills: _____

    Communication method: _____

Name 2: _____

    Knowledge/skills: _____

    Communication method: _____

Name 3: _____

    Knowledge/skills: _____

    Communication method: _____

Name 4: _____

    Knowledge/skills: _____

    Communication method: _____

Name 5: _____

    Knowledge/skills: _____

    Communication method: _____

Name 6: _____

    Knowledge/skills: _____

    Communication method: _____

EXPERTISE EXERCISE 21

DEVISING AN EXPERT ACTION PLAN

Select three of the seven expert characteristics summarized on page 123 that, if improved, could elevate your level of expertise. Devise a series of actions you will undertake to practice, develop, and improve each characteristic. Finally, identify a colleague with whom you can share your ideas and who will give you feedback.

Expert characteristic 1: _____

    Actions: _____

    _____

    _____

    Colleague: _____

Expert characteristic 2: _____

    Actions: _____

    _____

    _____

    Colleague: _____

Expert characteristic 3: _____

    Actions: _____

    _____

    _____

    Colleague: _____

SEVEN

NAVIGATING THE JOURNEY

Becoming expert is a journey. In many ways, it is like life itself. When does one stop being a child? When does one stop being a beginner? In some ways, never. There are traits we had as children that we still have today. There are characteristics we displayed on the first day in business that we still display today. This book describes the development of expertise as a series of steps: the first step a beginner, the last step an expert. As with any set of steps, however, we can go both up and down—or never move off the first step at all.

In chapter 1, "The Three Keys to Expertise," we examined three factors that determine how high you will climb on the steps of becoming expert:

- Experience
- Knowledge
- Skills

As you gain more experience, knowledge, and skills, your professional characteristics change in ways that improve your professional performance. When the majority of your characteristics are associated with a particular level of expertise, we say that you have achieved that level, whether it be that of beginner, capable, competent, proficient, or expert. But if you fail to learn from new experiences or to stay abreast of the latest information in your industry, or if you stop developing essential skills, you begin to lose expertise. If a rookie shows up with superior skills or knowledge, you can be outperformed. As a result, knowing how to navigate the journey toward becoming expert is important, as it allows you to continue to move forward. I hope you will also find, as most people do, that as you gain expertise and enjoy more success in your business, you also enjoy the journey more.

Becoming Experienced

Simply put, you cannot become an expert business professional without substantial experience in your industry. Little evidence supports the idea that a person with no experience in a field can consistently outperform an individual with extensive experience in that same field. To the contrary, research consistently reveals that it takes extensive experience—a minimum of ten years in most fields—to reach the level of expert.[1]

Experience can serve you in two ways: first, your business experiences offer a wealth of knowledge; second, it is in your experiences that you can most accurately assess your skills. Skills seldom improve with experience—that takes practice—but experience quickly informs you about the adequacy of the skills you presently possess and indicates which skills are needed for greater success.

Practical Knowledge: Making Experience, Not Waiting for It

While formal or theoretical knowledge has a cherished and valuable place in business, the practical knowledge earned through experience is more helpful in meeting the daily challenges and demands of work. Practical knowledge holds several advantages over theoretical knowledge in business. First, the source of practical knowledge is everyday experience. You can easily turn that knowledge around and apply it to recurring everyday problems. Second, it has significant personal meaning for you. Meaningful information is far easier to commit to memory and to recall for application to impending challenges than a set of facts or axioms isolated from experience.

Several strategies can help you use experience to move you along the journey toward becoming expert. Perhaps most obvious is to gain as many experiences as possible. But be smart. Seek only those experiences outside your normal course of responsibility that can supply you with useful, practical knowledge that you can use now or in the future to improve your performance. So first, you must know what areas of knowledge are most helpful to you. If you are in sales, for example, sitting in on a product design meeting may give you an insight that can eventually help you sell your products or services to clients. If you are managing a group of line workers, taking a turn on a shift may supply you with some much-needed information on the challenges your workers face. If you have limited experience in your organization, get to know people in departments outside yours. You may want to shadow others during their daily routines to gain more insight about your company's operations. Information from other parts of your organization may come to bear on decisions and actions in your department. Experiences with clients, suppliers, and other people outside your organization who play a significant role in your success also can prove valuable. Don't wait for experiences that happen *to* you, but rather make them happen *for* you.

Secondhand experience can also be highly instructive. Therefore, seek opportunities to listen to and discuss pertinent business experiences, decisions, and strategies with your peers—and even competitors. Professional organizations offer a wealth of knowledge based on the experiences of others. These "communities of practice" have the explicit mission of professional education and development for members.[2] They promote the exchange and dissemination of new information and time-tested knowledge through meetings, publications, and online resources.

Applied Skills

As a coach for several professional golfers, I've spent considerable time on the practice tee watching seasoned pros and promising newcomers. It is not unusual to see a promising prospect with impeccable technique impressively launching golf balls long and straight from the practice tee. There are no style points in golf, however, and you get little credit for how far you can hit the golf ball in practice. The bottom line in performance is outcome. During a performance, skills are called on to produce results. If these promising golfers cannot produce the golf shots that give them an outstanding score in a tournament, they will never move from prospect to proven professional.

It is the same in business. Executing your business skills produces results—good or bad. Environmental conditions such as equipment, business climate, and competition play a role in the results you achieve, but everyone faces pretty much the same conditions you face. The difference is largely the skills you bring to the table. People with better sales skills sell more. People with better managerial skills manage better. People with better production skills produce more efficiently. But it is only in the performance that the quality and appropriateness of those skills are tested.

Therefore, in your experiences identify the skills you need to be successful. Objectively and honestly assess your skills in terms of both their appropriateness in meeting your business performance demands and their level of quality during performance. If your performance is not where you want it to be, check your skills. Refer to expertise exercise 14, "Developing Your Critical Skills," in chapter 4, and ensure that the skills you believe are important to a superior performance are the skills you are developing.

Learning from Experience

Experience alone does not make people experts, regardless of their years in the field or reputation. Rather, the ability to learn from experience and correctly structure the knowledge gained from experience is what separates experts from routine performers.

A recent study of instructors and students at a U.S. Postal Service training center revealed some interesting insights into experience and expertise.[3] The researchers looked for two characteristics commonly associated with expertise: holistic perception and the use of abstract concepts. Initially, they found no evidence of either in the more experienced group. However, when they regrouped the participants based on performance, the higher performers showed evidence of both characteristics. This finding led to the conclusion that experience alone is not an indicator of expertise.

This was not a singular finding. Other research has shown that people thought to be experts do not necessarily or always outperform their peers—or even beginners. Experienced professionals were not able to outperform peers, and in some cases beginners, in areas such as computer programming, stock investments, and clinical psychology.[4]

Becoming Knowledgeable

That experts know a great deal is no surprise. "Knowledge is power" is a cliché that has gotten as much mileage as any and a great deal more than most. The secret to understanding the knowledge you need to increase your expertise is not simply to load your brain with as much information as it will hold. The amount is not what makes the difference.

More important than the amount of knowledge is the organization of that knowledge. That's right. Your expertise is more dependent on how you organize knowledge than how much knowledge you have. Here's why: When you organize knowledge in ways that make it more accessible, functional, and efficient, you are able to tap into your knowledge stores quickly, thoroughly, and effectively when the knowledge is most needed.[5] This is not to say that the amount of knowledge is unimportant, because experts know more about their business and the factors that influence it than anyone. But how much knowledge you have is not nearly as important as how much knowledge you *use* and to what effect.

So how can the organization of your knowledge be leveraged for greater effect? Part of the answer lies in your experience. As you gain experience, you begin to understand what information is most useful to you in your business decisions and actions. When you are capable, you begin to see similarities across contexts and start using strategic knowledge when making decisions. When you reach competence, you add the ability to distinguish the important from the unimportant, and you have a sense of timing and momentum in decision making and plan execution. Additionally, you are guided by the bigger picture of long-term plans and goals. All of these characteristics contribute to your ability to organize knowledge in useful ways.

Research reveals that, as expertise grows, the sources of knowledge begin to shift.[6] The extensive and specialized knowledge of experts is accumulated both through years of experience and from numerous sources.[7] In their book *Mavericks at Work, Fast Company* magazine editors William Taylor and Polly LaBarre make the following point: "One of the defining responsibilities of a 21st-century [business] leader is to attract the best ideas from the most people, wherever those people might be."[8] In my study of experts, I have found that they rely on four key sources in becoming knowledgeable:

- Wisdom gained through experience
- Networking and human interaction
- Formal education
- The written word[9]

Wisdom Gained Through Experience

As noted earlier, experience serves as a valued teacher and wonderful source of knowledge. I learned that experts, in fact, consider experience to be their most valued source of knowledge.[10] The process of trial and error that defines experience proves critical in identifying successful business practices. Additionally, the opportunity to grow and develop, discover new ideas, detect gaps and deficiencies in knowledge, and apply knowledge from other sources in a practical setting all contribute to the wisdom of an expert.[11]

Experienced individuals often reflect on previous experiences to evaluate their current knowledge and to target areas for improvement. Experience teaches us what we do well and what we need to improve, and offers insight into how we might become better. Experience is cumulative, so we strive to improve today over what we accomplished yesterday by making adjustments to yesterday's actions.

Networking and Human Interaction

When information holds meaning, we call it knowledge. Information is given meaning not only by us but also by others. We value knowledge not just for its own sake or what it means to us, but also for what it means to others. Therefore, it's not surprising that you can gain a great deal of knowledge from your interactions with others. Others may know something you'd like—or need—to know.

Thus, human interaction is an important source of knowledge. Your network of personal contacts is a potentially valuable stream of critical information you can use in professional pursuits. Collegial contacts, client interactions, competitor observations and discussions, and the interactive nature of conferences, seminars, and workshops are all significant resources experts use to build their professional networks of relationships.[12] It is the value of experience that explains the importance of peers as a knowledge source. Experience is a common denominator: The most important knowledge for experts is conceived and incubated in the practical actions and events of professional practice—their own or others'.

Experts also cite clients as a critically useful source of knowledge. By attentively listening, experts gain access to information that will allow them to better meet client needs and adapt to different styles and personalities. Similarly, observing and listening to competitors gives a different perspective to solving similar problems that experts face in the business world.

Professional conferences, workshops, seminars, and other such meetings offer a unique opportunity for human interaction and knowledge acquisition that cannot be found in other sources. In these meetings you can learn from those people who are successful in your industry. Professional meetings are fertile ground for new ideas and innovations that can propel your performance forward.

To gain maximum knowledge from your network of peers, clients, and competitors, interviewing is an essential skill. By asking questions, you can access knowledge from others, particularly clients and competitors. You will find that the more you interview other professionals, the more willing they will be to share information and the more you can learn from them. As with all skills, the more you practice interviewing, the better you become. When people perceive you as sincere in your desire to learn from them, they are more willing to share what they know—even competitors.

Formal Education

Few experts cite formal education such as college study and recognized certification programs as the reason for their success or even for supplying the basic knowledge from which they make their most important decisions. In fact, two leading technology entrepreneurs, Bill Gates and Steve Jobs, never completed a college degree. That is not to say that a college education is eschewed by all experts. To the contrary, the overwhelming majority of successful business professionals have completed one or more college degree programs.

Formal education can represent an important foundation and a continuing source of knowledge for your business decisions and actions. It can teach you how to research information and give you structure for which to organize discipline-based knowledge such as mathematics, science, language, history, and so on. Professionally oriented programs such as business management and accounting, rather than discipline-based programs such as economics and psychology, provide more than just foundational knowledge. They also supply entry-level occupational skills and perhaps even initial professional experience through internships.

Formal education is the foundational knowledge from which other knowledge can grow and develop. In terms of your development as an expert, think of your formal education as a good start. But don't be fooled into thinking that because you have a degree you will be successful. Even with a college degree, you still have much to learn, and the sooner you realize that, the sooner your real education can begin.

The Written Word

Those who have a thirst to learn make it a habit to read. Books, professional journals, magazines, the Internet, and the popular press all offer knowledge in a written format. Experts tend to be voracious readers. It is not a stretch to believe that one of the dividing lines between being proficient and expert is reading.

Reading gives you access to ideas, information, people, and places that may otherwise be far beyond your reach. The thoughts of business, political, or military leaders from eras long past as well as descriptions of the decision making or action initiatives in major contemporary innovations are accessible through the written word. You will never be able to discuss science with Marie Curie or negotiation strategies with John Rockefeller or business growth with Sam Walton; however, you can read about those people and the decisions they made and actions they took.

Professional and industry journals and magazines are valuable knowledge sources, particularly for the latest information affecting your business. You would be hard pressed to find an investment expert who did not read the *Wall Street Journal* or *Investor's Business Daily* regularly. These publications offer insights into thoughts and events that may influence decisions you need to make or actions you need to take. Additionally, you may gain insights into what is working (or not) for others and find new options in your own practices. Without industry sources it is virtually impossible to stay up to date with trends that will affect your business and you.

Reading is a major predictor of knowledge.[13] The more reading you do, the more you will learn and know. The more you know, the more able you are to appreciate and respond to a situation. One dedicated reader is Starbucks CEO Howard Schultz. To retain the spiritual experience of a trip to the Holy Land, he read Leon Uris's *The*

Haj. Reading *Memoirs of a Geisha* followed his trip to Japan, and Schultz read four separate biographies of Franklin Roosevelt after visiting the Roosevelt Memorial in Washington, DC. He confesses to being a voracious reader on airplanes, packing several books to ensure that he doesn't run out.[14]

Becoming Skillful

After an extensive review of decades of research, the leading authority on the development of expertise, Anders Ericsson, concluded that it takes at least ten years of deliberate practice to reach the skill level of an expert.[15] You must *purposely practice* and refine the requisite skills of a business or profession to improve your performance. The steady application of critical skills in the business environment hones the skill sets that build expert performance. New skills are seldom neat or tidy, or yield the results one hopes for, but you will never grow without attempting to master the skills you need to be successful. Without intentional attention to improvement, new skills seldom develop and old skills soon plateau. In Ericsson's words,

> The development of high levels of skill requires the acquisition of representations that allow efficient control and execution of performance, as well as mechanisms that support planning, reasoning, and evaluation that mediate further improvement and maintenance of high levels of performance. Deliberate practice activities must be tightly coordinated and focus sequentially on improving one specified aspect of performance at a time. Furthermore, the amount of deliberate practice needed to win at an international level is massive and intimidating.[16]

Mark Twain, as expert an orator as he was a writer, recognized the importance of preparation and practice. In his opinion, "that impromptu speech is most worth listening to which has been carefully prepared in private and tried on a plaster case or an empty chair or any other appreciative object that will keep quiet until the speaker has got his matter and his delivery limbered up so that they will seem impromptu to an audience."[17] What many believed came naturally to Twain was actually the result of years of deliberate practice. And so it is with the skills of an expert—so graceful, fluid, effortless, and effective are the skills of an expert that they seem as natural as breathing. But they are not; they were learned. And here is how they were learned.

Three Steps to Learning New Skills

We often believe that people more skillful than ourselves were either endowed with something we were not or they know something we don't. Of the two options, the second is more likely. Any skill that has been mastered by anyone was learned. Skills—all skills—are learned in three steps:

1. Gain a better understanding of how the skill is performed.

2. Practice with activities that specifically develop the skill and have a feedback component.

3. Develop automatic execution, or automaticity.

Let's take each step in turn.

First, you must have a clear understanding of the scope and sequence of the skill or concept to be learned. Put another way, you must clearly understand how this activity is done correctly. For example, if you are a sales professional who can benefit from being more skilled at cold-calling clients, you must first understand what constitutes a good cold call. *What* do you do first, second, third, and so forth, and *how* do you follow each of those procedures? This is where the knowledge sources discussed previously in this chapter become so critical. This is also where beginners start: with the accepted procedures of an activity. In large part beginners must follow procedures because they have yet to sufficiently practice their skills to attain mastery. But at every level of expertise, it is wise to revisit the fundamental components of your skills to ensure that you are performing each to the best of your ability.

Second, you must devote extensive time to activities that are goal oriented and in conditions similar to those found in the actual performance. Because practice is so essential to developing skills at the expert level of performance, the following section is devoted to the keys to quality practice.

Third, you develop automatic skill execution, or automaticity, when you attain a certain level of understanding and practice in a particular skill. At this step you can execute the skill with little or no conscious thought. Writing, walking, keyboarding, and driving an automobile are examples of skills automatically executed by many adults. The advantage of automaticity is that, during performance, you can concentrate on the purpose or goal of the performance without having to focus attention on the mechanics of the technique. The disadvantage is that once you can perform a skill automatically and are no longer giving it conscious attention, it becomes more difficult to modify it—and thus more difficult to improve it. That is not to say it is impossible to improve, but rather that it will take a great deal of focused practice to do so because you have reached a plateau in your performance.

Keys to Quality Practice

Here is a key you must not forget if you hope to become a better business professional:

> **Identify the one skill that, if improved, will make the biggest difference in your business success in the next six to twelve months.**

Why only one skill? If it will indeed make the biggest difference in your business performance, then no other skill can be more important, and therefore it deserves spending time developing this skill more. Focus on one skill until it's mastered and then, when you begin to get noticeable improvements in your performance, identify the next skill that will elevate your performance even more.

After you know which skill to improve, develop a practice strategy and a realistic schedule. Both the quality and quantity of practice matter. Just putting in hours of practice does not improve skills. Remember the earlier example of handwriting. Is it any better today than it was a year ago or five years ago? It may have even deteriorated. Repeating a skill with no effort or repeating activities to improve a skill does not lead to a better performance. Experience alone does not make you better at what you do.

Quality practice consists of methods and activities that lead directly to improvement in those skills that account for performance. If you set aside even a few minutes a week to practicing proper letter formation and use activities such as tracing over well-formed letters or words, your handwriting will improve. The same is true of any skill necessary for your business practice. If you practice your cold-calling technique with a colleague, or even a phantom client, several times before calling real clients, your cold-calling skills will improve. To be better tomorrow than you were yesterday requires intentional effort on your part today.

Activities that are practiced must be appropriate for your current business knowledge and skills. If the activities you select are ill-suited to you, no amount of practice time can possibly lead to improvement. Choose activities that are directly targeted at improving that key skill you identified earlier—the one that will have the biggest impact on your business performance. Practice activities that are well suited for a seasoned sales manager may not be appropriate for a beginner, so choose wisely. The differences in experience, knowledge, and skills are too great for the practice activity to benefit each level of expertise.

For example, if your organization is launching a new product, it is better for the novice salesperson to practice new presentations for colleagues before showing them to clients. The beginner is more able to accept feedback from colleagues and make adjustments to the presentations accordingly. Practicing before clients would make beginners too nervous and possibly defensive—and they would be unable to learn from the experience. However, seasoned professionals who are attempting to improve client interview skills may want to practice a new technique on established clients prior to facing potential clients. Most clients don't mind giving feedback about what they like or don't like about particular sales approaches, and proficient professionals have the skill and confidence to listen and learn from clients' comments.

A study at a music academy in Berlin, Germany, provides insightful guidance for the focused practice of experienced professionals. The violinists kept a diary of the time they spent each week on different activities. All groups of the violinists spent about the same amount of time (more than fifty hours) on music-related activities. The best violinists, however, spent more time per week on activities that were specifically designed to improve performance—for example, a solitary practice to master specific goals determined by their music teachers during weekly lessons.[18]

In addition, by focusing on practicing skills that have the most impact on performance, your quality-practice activities require your full concentration. Fatigue or boredom turns practice time into wasted time. Frequent breaks during practice help keep you fresh and alert. Short but frequent practice sessions yield better and faster results than a few marathon practice sessions.

In September 2004, Niclas Fasth and I sat watching an international golf championship, the Ryder Cup. Niclas had been a member of the previous and victorious 2002 European Ryder Cup team. But this year, he watched as others played. Niclas had competed full time on the PGA tour in the United States and had not played well enough to retain his playing privileges. I saw several reasons why Niclas hadn't played well: two bouts of the flu that affected his play for weeks, the jet lag from trips to and from his home in England and the United States, and the distraction of the birth of his second child.

Niclas, however, is not given to excuses. He does not brood about bad breaks or poor luck, and he never feels sorry for himself. Rather, he sees his destiny as resting firmly in his own hands and therefore constantly plans the future rather than lament the past. He writes out clear, specific goals that will lead him to success, and he regularly reviews them. He then sets up a practice plan to develop the skills and knowledge needed to improve his performance and achieve his goals. He regularly reviews this plan and makes changes when progress is wanting.

How much does Niclas practice? At the World Cup Championships on Kiawah Island, Niclas could be seen silhouetted against a setting sun as he continued practice until darkness prevented him from seeing the ball. A few months later, while I was having morning coffee with friends during the Deutsche Bank golf tournament, my cell phone rang just before 6:00 a.m. The sun was not even up. "Who would call you at this hour?" someone asked. "Niclas Fasth." I answered the phone and heard "Paul. This is Niclas. We're on our way to the practice tee. Can you join us there?"

Watching the 2004 Ryder Cup, Niclas was thinking ahead to 2005. How did 2005 end, and what did Niclas achieve? He finished thirteenth on the European Order of Merit (only twelve players had a better year), and he won—not once—but twice. Every year in the past three years, Niclas has won at least two tournaments on the European professional golf tour, placed second at the British Open Championship, placed fourth at the U.S. Open Championship directly behind Tiger Woods, and at the time of this writing is ranked twenty-first in the world. Why? He has clear goals, practices during uncommon hours, and has never lost faith in his ability to navigate his way to being the best he is capable of becoming—an expert. It is a formula that has served well those who reach the top of their field. It is a formula that will work for you, too.

Setting Your Course

So where to from here? Check back to pages 8–10 and review your score on expertise exercise 1, "Rating Your Expertise." This will give you a good indication of your present level. Begin there. Review the "Characteristics of the 5 Steps to Expert" table on page 144, focusing on your current level of expertise. Do you see characteristics in that level you may need to strengthen? You would be ill-advised to move to the next step until the step you are currently on is firmly in place. So review the expertise exercises you did in the chapter that corresponds to your current step, and make sure you have the experience, knowledge, and skills to advance to the next step. But also ask for honest feedback from trusted colleagues, seek knowledge you believe will help you perform at your best, and finally, enjoy the journey. Some people get a nosebleed when they climb too high, but experts enjoy both the challenge and the view in reaching the peak. See you at the top.

CHARACTERISTICS OF THE 5 STEPS TO EXPERT

1. Beginners

- Behave in ways that are rational, procedural, and inflexible
- Make decisions guided by rules and norms
- Do not feel responsible for the outcomes of their actions
- Lack comfortable, efficient routines for everyday tasks

2. Capable Performers

- Have functional skills and focus on task requirements
- See similarities across contexts
- Can make decisions in a timely manner
- Are responsive to situations
- Use strategic knowledge in decision making
- Learn best from experience but develop other resources as well

3. Competent Performers

- Use goals and long-term plans to guide decisions and actions
- Distinguish important from unimportant factors when analyzing situations or events
- Plan contingently
- Have a sense of timing and momentum in making decisions and taking actions

4. Proficient Performers

- Have a strong sense of personal responsibility
- Have highly developed perceptual skills
- Use efficient routines to handle everyday tasks
- Analyze and solve problems with forward thinking
- Predict future events with a high degree of accuracy

5. Experts

- Seek knowledge insatiably
- Have a superior memory
- Attend to the atypical
- Plan extensively and act intuitively
- Execute skills gracefully and automatically
- Meet inadequacies and failures with corrective action
- Are self-monitoring

AFTERWORD

Research has conclusively shown that experts are made, not born. Expertise is not the manifestation of innate traits or qualities nor does it come from possessing certain personality characteristics, physical attributes, or intellectual powers. Rather, it is earned from years of experience in the workplace, the acquisition of extensive knowledge of all the factors that shape the ultimate outcome of one's performance, and the deliberate practice of essential skills. Not everyone can become *the* top performer in their field, but everyone can increase their expertise and thus become better at what they do—even experts. Five steps will take you from business novice to elite performer. In developing expertise, take each step in turn. There is no other way. In so doing, you will climb higher in your pursuit of expertise. In the words of Henry Wadsworth Longfellow,

> *The heights by great men reached and kept*
> *Were not attained by sudden flight,*
> *But they, while their companions slept,*
> *Were toiling upward in the night.*

NOTES

Preface
1. See Kristen Heflin, "An Expert on Expertise," *Education* (2005): 15.
2. Jeff Thull, *Exceptional Selling* (New York: Wiley, 2006), 11.

Introduction
1. John Wooden and Steve Jamison, *My Personal Best: Life Lessons from an All-American Journey* (New York: McGraw-Hill, 2004), 86–87.
2. John Wooden, www.coachjohnwooden.com.
3. Charles O'Reilly, "Winning the Career Tournament," *Fast Company* (January 2004), www.fastcompany.com/articles/2004/01/oreilly/.
4. Hubert L. Dreyfus, *What Computers Can't Do: A Critique of Artificial Reason* (New York: Harper, 1972).

Chapter 1
1. Bob Danzig, *Conversations with Bobby: From Foster Child to Corporate Executive* (Arlington, VA: CWLA Press, 2007), 29–30.
2. Peter Drucker, *The Effective Executive* (New York: Harper & Row, 1966), 22–23.
3. Sabine Sonnetag, "Expertise in Professional Software Design: A Process Study," *Journal of Applied Psychology* 83 (1998): 703–715.
4. K. Anders Ericsson et al., eds., *The Cambridge Handbook of Expertise and Expert Performance* (New York: Cambridge University Press, 2006), 698.

5. See Mark Smith, "Lesson from Sidelines Past: A Story of Bobby Bowden" (unpublished doctoral dissertation, University of Georgia, Athens, 2004), 64.

6. See Bernard Avishai, "A European Platform for Global Competition: An Interview with VW's Carl Hahn," *Harvard Business Review* (July–August 1991): 2–11.

7. Paul Feltovich, Michael Prietula, and K. Anders Ericsson, "Studies in Expertise from Psychological Perspectives," in *The Cambridge Handbook of Expertise and Expert Performance*, ed. Ericsson et al., 41–67.

8. Eleanor Maguire et al., "Routes to Remembering: The Brains Behind Superior Memory," *Nature Neuroscience* 6 (2003): 90–95.

9. Michelene Chi, Robert Glaser, and Marshall Farr, *The Nature of Expertise* (Hillsdale, NJ: Lawrence Erlbaum, 1988), 129.

10. William Chase, ed., *Visual Information Processing* (New York: Academic Press, 1973).

11. Paul Schempp et al., "Subject Expertise and Teachers' Knowledge," *Journal of Teaching in Physical Education* 17 (1998): 342–356.

12. See William O'Neil, *Business Leaders and Success* (New York: McGraw-Hill, 2004), 47.

13. Fons Trompenaars, *21 Leaders for the 21st Century: How Innovative Leaders Manage in the Digital Age* (New York: McGraw-Hill, 2001).

14. John Maxwell, *The 21 Irrefutable Laws of Leadership: Follow Them and People Will Follow You* (Nashville, TN: Thomas Nelson, 2007); Morey Stettner, *Skills for New Managers* (New York: McGraw-Hill, 2000); Jack Canfield and Janet Switzer, *The Success Principles: How to Get from Where You Are to Where You Want to Be* (New York: HarperCollins, 2006); Donald Mitchell et al., *The Ultimate Competitive Advantage: Secrets of Continuously Developing a More Profitable Business Model* (San Francisco: Berrett-Koehler, 2003).

15. Gary Klein, *Sources of Power: How People Make Decisions* (Cambridge, MA: MIT Press, 1998).

Chapter 2

1. "Seven Steps to Sales Success," http://h30267.www3.hp.com/ecasts/oct05/selling_digital_7steps.html.

2. Ray Alcorn, "Top 5 Mistakes of Beginning Commercial Real Estate Investors" (2008), www.creonline.com/articles/art-318.html.

3. Marvin Traub, *Like No Other Store . . . : The Bloomingdale's Legend and the Revolution in American Marketing* (New York: Random House, 1993), 46.

4. See "Forecasters: Katrina to Aim for Mississippi and Louisiana," CNN.com (August 26, 2005), www.cnn.com/2005/weather/08/06/tropical.weather/index.html.

5. See "'Can I Quit Now?' FEMA Chief Wrote as Katrina Raged," CNN.com (November 4, 2005), www.cnn.com/2005/US/11/03/brown.fema.emails.
6. Joseph Baker, Jean Côté, and Janice Deakin, "Cognitive Characteristics of Expert, Middle of the Pack and Back of the Pack Ultra-Endurance Triathletes," *Psychology of Sport and Exercise* 6 (2005): 551–558.
7. O'Neil, *Business Leaders and Success,* 14.

Chapter 3
1. Jim Collins, *Good to Great: Why Some Companies Make the Leap . . . and Others Don't* (New York: HarperCollins, 2001), 20.
2. See Rodd Wagner and James K. Harter, *12: The Elements of Great Managing* (New York: Gallup Press, 2006), 111.
3. Sonnetag, "Expertise in Professional Software Design," 703–715.
4. See Julie Fenster, *In the Words of Great Business Leaders* (New York: Wiley, 2000), 121.
5. Michelene Chi, Paul Feltovich, and Robert Glaser, "Categorization and Representation of Physics Problems by Experts and Novices," *Cognitive Science* 5 (1981): 130.
6. See O'Neil, *Business Leaders and Success,* 47.
7. Rhona Flin, Georgina Slaven, and Keith Stewart, "Emergency Decision Making in the Offshore Oil and Gas Industry," *Human Factors* 38 (1996): 262–277.
8. Klein, *Sources of Power.*
9. Rita Levi-Montalcini, *In Praise of Imperfection: My Life and Work* (New York: Basic Books, 1989).
10. Ann B. Graham and Vincent G. Pizzo, "A Question of Balance: Case Studies in Strategic Knowledge Management," in *The Strategic Management of Intellectual Capital: Resources for the Knowledge-Based Economy,* ed. David Klein (Oxford, England: Butterworth-Heineman, 1997), 22.
11. Harish Sujan, Mita Sujan, and James R. Bettman, "Knowledge Structure Differences Between More Effective and Less Effective Salespeople," *Journal of Marketing Research* 25 (1988): 81–86.
12. Mark P. Higgins and Mary P. Tully, "Hospital Doctors and Their Schemas About Appropriate Prescribing," *Medical Education* 39 (2005): 184–193.
13. Timm Kainen, "Who Succeeds in the Murky Middle?" *Journal of Applied Business Research* 23, no. 4 (2007): 61–68.

Chapter 4
1. Southwest Airlines Web site, http://southwest.com/about_swa/mission.html.
2. See Kevin Frieberg and Jackie Frieberg, *Nuts! Southwest Airlines' Crazy Recipe for Business and Personal Success* (New York: Broadway Books, 1996).
3. See Jon Meacham, *Franklin and Winston: An Intimate Portrait of an Epic Friendship* (New York: Random House, 2004), 285.

4. Drucker, *The Effective Executive*, 123.
5. Mica Endsley, "Toward a Theory of Situation Awareness in Dynamic Systems," *Human Factors* 37 (1995): 32–64.
6. Janet Davidson and Robert Sternberg, *The Psychology of Problem Solving* (New York: Cambridge University Press, 2003).
7. D. Floyd Jones, Lynn Housner, and Alan Kornspan, "Interactive Decision Making and Behavior of Experienced and Inexperienced Basketball Coaches During Practice," *Journal of Teaching in Physical Education* 64 (1997): 454–468.
8. Stephen Covey, *The 7 Habits of Highly Effective People* (New York: Simon & Schuster, 1989), 98.
9. Leaders & Success, *Investor's Business Daily*, November 16, 2006, A3.
10. Sophie Woorons, "An Analysis of Expert and Novice Tennis Instructors' Perceptual Capacities" (doctoral dissertation, University of Georgia, Athens, 2001), 85.
11. Beth Adelson, "When Novices Surpass Experts: The Difficulty of a Task May Increase with Expertise," *Journal of Experimental Psychology* 10 (1984): 494.
12. Carolyn Prince and Eduardo Salas, "Situation Assessment for Routine Flight and Decision Making," *International Journal of Cognitive Ergonomics* 1 (1998): 315–324.
13. Fenster, *In the Words of Great Business Leaders*, 33.
14. Thull, *Exceptional Selling*, 59.
15. Robert Shook, *The Greatest Sales Stories Ever Told: From the World's Best Salespeople* (New York: McGraw-Hill, 1997).
16. See Noel Tichy and Ram Charan, "Speed, Simplicity, Self-Confidence: An Interview with Jack Welch," *Harvard Business Review* 28, no. 4 (1989): 113–114.

Chapter 5

1. Collins, *Good to Great*, 34.
2. Mark Sanborn, *The Fred Factor* (New York: Doubleday, 2004), 8–9.
3. James Gleick, *Genius: The Life and Science of Richard Feynman* (New York: Vintage Books, 1992), 215.
4. See Bryan McCullick, Russell Cummings, and Paul Schempp, "The Professional Orientations of Expert Golf Instructors," *International Journal of Physical Education* 36 (1999): 22.
5. Mica Endsley and Chris Bolstad, "Individual Differences in Pilot Situational Awareness," *International Journal of Aviation Psychology* 4 (1994): 241–264.
6. Richard M. Rosen and Fred Adair, "CEOs Misperceive Top Teams' Performance," *Harvard Business Review* (September 2007): 30.
7. Fenster, *In the Words of Great Business Leaders*, 88.
8. Bent Peterson and Torbin Pederson, "Coping with Liability of Foreignness: Different Learning Engagements of Entrant Firms," *Journal of International Business Management* 8, no. 3 (2002): 339–350.

9. John R. Anderson, *The Architecture of Cognition* (Cambridge, MA: Harvard University Press, 1983).

10. Robert E. Christensen, Michael D. Fetters, and Lee A. Green, "Opening the Black Box: Cognitive Strategies in Family Practice," *Annals of Family Medicine* 3 (2005): 144–150.

11. Vimla Patel and Guy J. Groen, "The General and Specific Nature of Medical Expertise: A Critical Look," in *Toward a General Theory of Expertise: Prospects and Limits,* ed. K. Anders Ericsson and Jacqui Smith (New York: Cambridge University Press, 1991), 93–125.

12. Ericsson et al., eds., *Cambridge Handbook of Expertise and Expert Performance.*

13. Jos Arts, Wim Gijselaers, and Henny Boshuizen, "Understanding Managerial Problem-Solving," *Contemporary Educational Psychology* 31 (2006): 387–410.

14. Chi, Feltovich, and Glaser, "Categorization and Representation of Physics Problems by Experts and Novices," 121–152.

15. See Fenster, *In the Words of Great Business Leaders,* 322.

16. Kathy Carter et al., "Processing and Using Information About Students: A Study of Expert, Novice, and Postulant Teachers," *Teaching and Teacher Education* 3 (1987): 147–157.

17. Tim Gabbett et al., "Testing and Training Anticipation Skills in Softball Fielders," *International Journal of Sports Science and Coaching* 2 (2007): 15–24.

Chapter 6

1. Paul Schempp, "Where Experts Find Answers," *American Society for Training and Development Research-to-Practice Conference Proceedings* (Alexandria, VA: ASTD, 2006).

2. See Fenster, *In the Words of Great Business Leaders,* 16.

3. Brousseau, Kenneth, et al., "The Seasoned Executive's Decision-Making Style," *Harvard Business Review* 84, no. 2 (2006): 110–121.

4. Covey, *The 7 Habits of Highly Effective People,* 240.

5. Ibid., 241.

6. Schempp et al., "Subject Expertise and Teachers' Knowledge," 342–356.

7. See Smith, "Lessons from Sidelines Past," 232.

8. Collins, *Good to Great,* 154.

9. K. Anders Ericsson et al., "Uncovering the Structure of a Memorist's Superior 'Basic' Memory Capacity," *Cognitive Psychology* 49 (2004): 191–238.

10. Mark Cuban, "Success and Motivation, Part 3," May 7, 2004, www.blogmaverick.com.

11. Mark Cuban, "Success and Motivation, Almost Part 2," April 25, 2004, www.blogmaverick.com.

12. Ericsson et al., "Uncovering the Structure of a Memorist's Superior 'Basic' Memory Capacity."

13. Bryan McCullick et al., "An Analysis of the Working Memory of Expert Sport Instructors," *Journal of Teaching in Physical Education* 25 (2006): 149–165.
14. Alan Casel, "Does Expertise Reduce Age Differences in Recall Memory?" *Journals of Gerontology Series B: Psychological Sciences and Social Sciences* 62 (2007): 194–196.
15. Jeffrey Gangemi, "Nobel Winner Yunus: Microcredit Missionary," *Business-Week*, December 26, 2005.
16. O'Neil, *Business Leaders and Success*, 65.
17. Dean Smith, with John Kilgo and Sally Jenkins, *A Coach's Life* (New York: Random House, 1999).
18. Wooden and Jamison, *My Personal Best.*
19. Neil Charness, "Age and Skilled Problem Solving," *Journal of Experimental Psychology: General* 110 (1981): 21–38.
20. Ericsson et al., eds., *Cambridge Handbook of Expertise and Expert Performance*, 233.
21. Vimla Patel, David Evans, and Guy Groen, "Diagnostic Reasoning and Expertise," *Psychology of Learning and Motivation* 31 (1989): 137–252.
22. Franz Humer, "Intuition," *Harvard Business Review* 85, no. 1 (2007): 17–18.
23. Ibid., 18.
24. Benjamin Bloom, "Automaticity," *Educational Leadership* (February 1986): 70–77.
25. Ibid.
26. Linda Hill, "Becoming the BOSS," *Harvard Business Review* 85, no. 1 (2007): 48–56.
27. See Michael Schrage, "A Japanese Giant Rethinks Globalization: An Interview with Yoshibisa Tabuchi," in *Leaders on Leadership: Interviews with Top Executives*, ed. Warren Bennis, Harvard Business Review Book Series (Boston: Bennis, 1992), 115.
28. K. Anders Ericsson, "The Scientific Study of Expert Levels of Performance: General Implications for Optimal Learning and Creativity," *High Ability Studies* 9 (1998): 75–100.
29. Ericsson et al., eds., *Cambridge Handbook of Expertise and Expert Performance*, 45.
30. Ericsson, "The Scientific Study of Expert Levels of Performance."
31. See Jack Canfield and Mark Victor Hansen, *Chicken Soup for the Soul: Inspirational Stories, Powerful Principles, and Practical Techniques to Help You Make Your Dreams Come True* (Deerfield Beach, FL: HCI, 2003), 73.
32. Leaders & Success, *Investor's Business Daily*, November 10, 2006, A3.
33. Schempp et al., "Subject Expertise and Teachers' Knowledge."
34. Barry Zimmerman and Anastasia Kitsantas, "Self-Regulated Learning of a Motoric Skill: The Role of Goal Setting and Self-Monitoring," *Journal of Applied Sport Psychology* 8 (1996): 60–75.

35. Paul Karoly, "Mechanisms of Self-Regulation: A Systems View," *Annual Review of Psychology* 44 (1993): 23–52.

36. Ibid.

37. See William Y. Lan and Jake Morgan, "Videotaping as a Means of Self-Monitoring to Improve Theater Students' Performance," *Journal of Experimental Education* 71 (2003): 371–381; William Y. Lan, "The Effects of Self-Monitoring on Students' Course Performance, Use of Learning Strategies, Attitude, Self-Judgment Ability, and Knowledge Representation," *Journal of Experimental Education* 64 (1996): 101–115; Zimmerman and Kitsantas, "Self-Regulated Learning of a Motoric Skill."

38. Chi et al., "Categorization and Representation of Physics Problems by Experts and Novices."

39. Chi, Glaser, and Farr, *The Nature of Expertise*, xx.

40. Paul Schempp, "The Self-Monitoring of Expert Sport Instructors," *International Journal of Sport Science & Coaching* 1 (2006): 25–35.

41. See O'Neil, *Business Leaders and Success*, 48.

Chapter 7

1. Ericsson, "The Scientific Study of Expert Levels of Performance."

2. Etienne Wenger and William M. Snyder, "Communities of Practice: The Organizational Frontier," *Harvard Business Review* (January–February 2000): 139–145.

3. John Bradley, Ravi Paul, and Elaine Seeman, "Analyzing the Structure of Expert Knowledge," *Information & Management* 43 (2006): 77–91.

4. Ericsson et al., eds., *Cambridge Handbook of Expertise and Expert Performance*, 398.

5. Jean Bedard and Michelene Chi, "Expertise," *Current Directions in Psychological Science* 1, no. 4 (1992): 135–139.

6. K. Anders Ericsson, "Deliberate Practice and the Acquisition of and Maintenance of Expert Performance in Medicine and Related Domains," *Academic Medicine* 10 (2004): S1–S12.

7. Daniel Gould et al., "Educational Needs of Elite US National Team, Pan American, and Olympic Coaches," *Journal of Teaching in Physical Education* 9 (1990): 332–344.

8. William Taylor and Polly LaBarre, *Mavericks at Work: Why the Most Original Minds in Business Win* (New York: HarperCollins, 2006), 73.

9. Schempp, "Where Experts Find Answers," 146.

10. Paul Schempp, "Learning on the Job: An Analysis of the Acquisition of a Teacher's Knowledge," *Journal of Research and Development in Education* 28 (1995): 237–244.

11. Schempp, "Where Experts Find Answers," 146.

12. Ibid., 146.

13. Keith E. Stanovich and Anne E. Cunningham, "Where Does Knowledge Come From? Specific Associations Between Print Exposure and Information Acquisition," *Journal of Educational Psychology* 85 (1993): 211–229.
14. O'Neil, *Business Leaders and Success,* 171.
15. Ericsson, "Deliberate Practice and the Acquisition of and Maintenance of Expert Performance in Medicine and Related Domains," S1–S12.
16. K. Anders Ericsson, "Recent Advances in Expertise Research: A Commentary on the Contributions to the Special Issue," *Applied Cognitive Psychology* 19 (2005): 238.
17. See Alex Ayers, ed., *The Wit and Wisdom of Mark Twain* (New York: Meridian, 1984), 219.
18. K. Anders Ericsson, Ralf Th. Krampe, and Clements Tesch-Römer, "The Role of Deliberate Practice in the Acquisition of Expert Performance," *Psychological Review* 100 (1993): 363–406.

REFERENCES

Adelson, Beth. "When Novices Surpass Experts: The Difficulty of a Task May Increase with Expertise." *Journal of Experimental Psychology* 10 (1984): 494.

Anderson, John R. *The Architecture of Cognition.* Cambridge, MA: Harvard University Press, 1983.

Arts, Jos, Wim Gijselaers, and Henny Boshuizen. "Understanding Managerial Problem-Solving." *Contemporary Educational Psychology* 31 (2006): 387–410.

Avishai, Bernard. "A European Platform for Global Competition: An Interview with VW's Carl Hahn." *Harvard Business Review* (July–August 1991): 2–11.

Ayers, Alex, ed. *The Wit and Wisdom of Mark Twain.* New York: Meridian, 1984.

Baker, Joseph, Jean Côté, and Janice Deakin. "Cognitive Characteristics of Expert, Middle of the Pack and Back of the Pack Ultra-Endurance Triathletes." *Psychology of Sport and Exercise* 6 (2005): 551–558.

Bedard, Jean and Michelene Chi. "Expertise." *Current Directions in Psychological Science* 1, no. 4 (1992): 135–139.

Bloom, Benjamin. "Automaticity." *Educational Leadership* (February 1986): 70–77.

Bradley, John, Ravi Paul, and Elaine Seeman. "Analyzing the Structure of Expert Knowledge." *Information & Management* 43 (2006): 77–91.

Brousseau, Kenneth, Michael Driver, Gary Hourihan, and Rikard Larsen. "The Seasoned Executive's Decision-Making Style." *Harvard Business Review* 84 no. 2 (2006): 110–121.

Canfield, Jack, and Mark Victor Hansen. *Chicken Soup for the Soul: Inspirational Stories, Powerful Principles, and Practical Techniques to Help You Make Your Dreams Come True.* Deerfield Beach, FL: HCI, 2003.

Canfield, Jack, and Janet Switzer. *The Success Principles: How to Get from Where You Are to Where You Want to Be.* New York: HarperCollins, 2006.

Carter, Kathy, Donna Sabers, Katherine Cushing, Stefinee Pinnegar, and David Berliner. "Processing and Using Information About Students: A Study of Expert, Novice, and Postulant Teachers." *Teaching and Teacher Education* 3 (1987): 147–157.

Casel, Alan. "Does Expertise Reduce Age Differences in Recall Memory?" *Journals of Gerontology Series B: Psychological Sciences and Social Sciences* 62 (2007): 194–196.

Charness, Neil. "Age and Skilled Problem Solving." *Journal of Experimental Psychology: General* 110 (1981): 21–38.

Chase, William, ed. *Visual Information Processing.* New York: Academic Press, 1973.

Chi, Michelene, Paul Feltovich, and Robert Glaser. "Categorization and Representation of Physics Problems by Experts and Novices." *Cognitive Science* 5 (1981): 130.

Chi, Michelene, Robert Glaser, and Marshall Farr. *The Nature of Expertise.* Hillsdale, NJ: Lawrence Erlbaum, 1988.

Christensen, Robert E., Michael D. Fetters, and Lee A. Green. "Opening the Black Box: Cognitive Strategies in Family Practice." *Annals of Family Medicine* 3 (2005): 144–150.

Collins, Jim. *Good to Great: Why Some Companies Make the Leap . . . and Others Don't.* New York: HarperCollins, 2001.

Covey, Stephen. *The 7 Habits of Highly Effective People.* New York: Simon & Schuster, 1989.

Cuban, Mark. "Success and Motivation, Almost Part 2." April 25, 2004, www.blogmaverick.com.

Cuban, Mark. "Success and Motivation, Part 3." May 7, 2004, www.blogmaverick.com.

Danzig, Bob. *Conversations with Bobby: From Foster Child to Corporate Executive.* Arlington, VA: CWLA Press, 2007.

Davidson, Janet, and Robert Sternberg. *The Psychology of Problem Solving.* New York: Cambridge University Press, 2003.

Dreyfus, Hubert L. *What Computers Can't Do: A Critique of Artificial Reason.* New York: Harper & Row, 1972.

Drucker, Peter. *The Effective Executive.* New York: Harper & Row, 1966.

Endsley, Mica. "Toward a Theory of Situation Awareness in Dynamic Systems." *Human Factors* 37 (1995): 32–64.

Endsley, Mica, and Chris Bolstad. "Individual Differences in Pilot Situational Awareness." *International Journal of Aviation Psychology* 4 (1994): 241–264.

Ericsson, K. Anders. "The Scientific Study of Expert Levels of Performance: General Implications for Optimal Learning and Creativity." *High Ability Studies* 9 (1998): 75–100.

Ericsson, K. Anders. "Deliberate Practice and the Acquisition of and Maintenance of Expert Performance in Medicine and Related Domains." *Academic Medicine* 10 (2004): S1–S12.

Ericsson, K. Anders. "Recent Advances in Expertise Research: A Commentary on the Contributions to the Special Issue." *Applied Cognitive Psychology* 19 (2005): 238.

Ericsson, K. Anders, Neil Charness, Paul Feltovich, and Robert Hoffman, eds. *The Cambridge Handbook of Expertise and Expert Performance.* New York: Cambridge University Press, 2006.

Ericsson, K. Anders, Peter Delaney, George Weaver, and Rajan Mahadevan. "Uncovering the Structure of a Memorist's Superior 'Basic' Memory Capacity." *Cognitive Psychology* 49 (2004): 191–238.

Ericsson, K. Anders, Ralf Th. Krampe, and Clements Tesch-Römer. "The Role of Deliberate Practice in the Acquisition of Expert Performance." *Psychological Review* 100 (1993): 363–406.

Fenster, Julie. *In the Words of Great Business Leaders.* New York: Wiley, 2000.

Flin, Rhona, Georgina Slaven, and Keith Stewart. "Emergency Decision Making in the Offshore Oil and Gas Industry." *Human Factors* 38 (1996): 262–277.

Frieberg, Kevin, and Jackie Frieberg. *Nuts! Southwest Airlines' Crazy Recipe for Business and Personal Success.* New York: Broadway Books, 1996.

Gabbett, Tim, Martin Rubinoff, Lachian Thorbum, and Damian Farrow. "Testing and Training Anticipation Skills in Softball Fielders." *International Journal of Sports Science and Coaching* 2 (2007): 15–24.

Gangemi, Jeffrey. "Nobel Winner Yunus: Microcredit Missionary," *BusinessWeek,* December 26, 2005.

Gleick, James. *Genius: The Life and Science of Richard Feynman.* New York: Vintage Books, 1992.

Gould, Daniel, et al. "Educational Needs of Elite US National Team, Pan American, and Olympic Coaches," *Journal of Teaching in Physical Education* 9 (1990): 332–344.

Graham, Ann B., and Vincent G. Pizzo. "A Question of Balance: Case Studies in Strategic Knowledge Management." In *The Strategic Management of Intellectual Capital: Resources for the Knowledge-Based Economy.* Edited by David Klein. Oxford, England: Butterworth-Heineman, 1997.

Heflin, Kristen. "An Expert on Expertise." *Education* (2005): 15.

Higgins, Mark P., and Mary P. Tully. "Hospital Doctors and Their Schemas About Appropriate Prescribing." *Medical Education* 39 (2005): 184–193.

Hill, Linda. "Becoming the BOSS." *Harvard Business Review* 85, no. 1 (2007): 48–56.

Humer, Franz. "Intuition." *Harvard Business Review* 85, no. 1 (2007): 17–18.

Jones, D. Floyd, Lynn Housner, and Alan Kornspan. "Interactive Decision Making and Behavior of Experienced and Inexperienced Basketball Coaches During Practice." *Journal of Teaching in Physical Education* 64 (1997): 454–468.

Kainen, Timm. "Who Succeeds in the Murky Middle?" *Journal of Applied Business Research* 23, no. 4 (2007): 61–68.

Karoly, Paul. "Mechanisms of Self-Regulation: A Systems View." *Annual Review of Psychology* 44 (1993): 23–52.

Klein, Gary. *Sources of Power: How People Make Decisions.* Cambridge, MA: MIT Press, 1998.

Lan, William Y. "The Effects of Self-Monitoring on Students' Course Performance, Use of Learning Strategies, Attitude, Self-Judgment Ability, and Knowledge Representation." *Journal of Experimental Education* 64 (1996): 101–115.

Lan, William Y., and Jake Morgan. "Videotaping as a Means of Self-Monitoring to Improve Theater Students' Performance." *Journal of Experimental Education* 71 (2003): 371–381.

Levi-Montalcini, Rita. *In Praise of Imperfection: My Life and Work.* New York: Basic Books, 1989.

Maguire, Eleanor, Elizabeth Valentine, John Wilding, and Narinder Kapur. "Routes to Remembering: The Brains Behind Superior Memory." *Nature Neuroscience* 6 (2003): 90–95.

Maxwell, John. *The 21 Irrefutable Laws of Leadership: Follow Them and People Will Follow You.* Nashville, TN: Thomas Nelson, 2007.

McCullick, Bryan, Russell Cummings, and Paul Schempp. "The Professional Orientations of Expert Golf Instructors." *International Journal of Physical Education* 36 (1999): 15–24.

McCullick, Bryan, Paul Schempp, Tiffany Tsu, Jinhong Jung, Brad Vickers, and Greg Schuknecht. "An Analysis of the Working Memory of Expert Sport Instructors." *Journal of Teaching in Physical Education* 25 (2006): 149–165.

Meacham, Jon. *Franklin and Winston: An Intimate Portrait of an Epic Friendship.* New York: Random House, 2004.

Mitchell, Donald, Carol Coles, B. Thomas Golisano, and Robert Knutson. *The Ultimate Competitive Advantage: Secrets of Continuously Developing a More Profitable Business Model.* San Francisco: Berrett-Koehler, 2003.

O'Neil, William. *Business Leaders and Success.* New York: McGraw-Hill, 2004.

O'Reilly, Charles. "Winning the Career Tournament." *Fast Company* (January 2004), www.fastcompany.com/articles/2004/01/oreilly/.

Patel, Vimla, David Evans, and Guy Groen. "Diagnostic Reasoning and Expertise." *Psychology of Learning and Motivation* 31 (1989): 137–252.

Patel, Vimla, and Guy J. Groen. "The General and Specific Nature of Medical Expertise: A Critical Look." In *Toward a General Theory of Expertise: Prospects and Limits.* Edited by K. Anders Ericsson and Jacqui Smith, pp. 93–125. New York: Cambridge University Press, 1991.

Peterson, Bent, and Torbin Pederson. "Coping with Liability of Foreignness: Different Learning Engagements of Entrant Firms." *Journal of International Business Management* 8, no. 3 (2002): 339–350.

Prince, Carolyn, and Eduardo Salas. "Situation Assessment for Routine Flight and Decision Making." *International Journal of Cognitive Ergonomics* 1 (1998): 315–324.

Rosen, Richard M., and Fred Adair. "CEOs Misperceive Top Teams' Performance." *Harvard Business Review* 85, no. 9 (September 2007): 30.

Sanborn, Mark. *The Fred Factor.* New York: Doubleday, 2004.

Schempp, Paul. "Learning on the Job: An Analysis of the Acquisition of a Teacher's Knowledge." *Journal of Research and Development in Education* 28 (1995): 237–244.

Schempp, Paul. "Where Experts Find Answers." *American Society for Training and Development Research-to-Practice Conference Proceedings.* Alexandria, VA: ASTD, 2006, 143–152.

Schempp, Paul, Dean Manross, Steven Tan, and Matthew Fincher. "Subject Expertise and Teachers' Knowledge." *Journal of Teaching in Physical Education* 17 (1998): 342–356.

Schempp, Paul, Bryan McCullick, Chris Busch, Collin Webster, and Ilse Mason. "The Self-Monitoring of Expert Sport Instructors." *International Journal of Sport Science & Coaching* 1 (2006): 25–35.

Schrage, Michael. "A Japanese Giant Rethinks Globalization: An Interview with Yoshibisa Tabuchi." In *Leaders on Leadership: Interviews with Top Executives.* Edited by Warren Bennis, Harvard Business Review Book Series. Boston: Bennis, 1992.

Shook, Robert. *The Greatest Sales Stories Ever Told: From the World's Best Salespeople.* New York: McGraw-Hill, 1997.

Smith, Dean, with John Kilgo and Sally Jenkins. *A Coach's Life.* New York: Random House, 1999.

Smith, Mark. "Lesson from Sidelines Past: A Story of Bobby Bowden." Unpublished doctoral dissertation, University of Georgia, Athens, 2004.

Sonnetag, Sabine. "Expertise in Professional Software Design: A Process Study." *Journal of Applied Psychology* 83 (1998): 703–715.

Stanovich, Keith E., and Anne E. Cunningham. "Where Does Knowledge Come From? Specific Associations Between Print Exposure and Information Acquisition." *Journal of Educational Psychology* 85 (1993): 211–229.

Stettner, Morey. *Skills for New Managers*. New York: McGraw-Hill, 2000.

Sujan, Harish, Mita Sujan, and James R. Bettman. "Knowledge Structure Differences Between More Effective and Less Effective Salespeople." *Journal of Marketing Research* 25 (1988): 81–86.

Taylor, William, and Polly LaBarre. *Mavericks at Work: Why the Most Original Minds in Business Win*. New York: HarperCollins, 2006.

Thull, Jeff. *Exceptional Selling*. New York: Wiley, 2006.

Tichy, Noel, and Ram Charan. "Speed, Simplicity, Self-Confidence: An Interview with Jack Welch." *Harvard Business Review* 28, no. 4 (1989): 113–114.

Traub, Marvin. *Like No Other Store . . . : The Bloomingdale's Legend and the Revolution in American Marketing*. New York: Random House, 1993.

Trompenaars, Fons. *21 Leaders for the 21st Century: How Innovative Leaders Manage in the Digital Age*. New York: McGraw-Hill, 2001.

Wagner, Rodd, and James K. Harter. *12: The Elements of Great Managing*. New York: Gallup Press, 2006.

Wenger, Etienne, and William M. Snyder. "Communities of Practice: The Organizational Frontier." *Harvard Business Review* (January–February 2000): 139–145.

Wooden, John, and Steve Jamison. *My Personal Best: Life Lessons from an All-American Journey*. New York: McGraw-Hill, 2004.

Woorons, Sophie. "An Analysis of Expert and Novice Tennis Instructors' Perceptual Capacities." Doctoral dissertation, University of Georgia, Athens, 2001.

Zimmerman, Barry, and Anastasia Kitsantas. "Self-Regulated Learning of a Motoric Skill: The Role of Goal Setting and Self-Monitoring." *Journal of Applied Sport Psychology* 8 (1996): 60–75.

INDEX

abstract thought processes, 66–67

action planning, 126

action taking: by capable performers, 52; by competent performers, 61–64, 69–72; by experts, 19; goals and long-term plans used in, 61–64, 75; intuitive, 111–113; momentum and timing used in, 69–72

Adelson, Beth, 66–67

anticipatory skills, 92

asking for help, 38–39

automatic behavior, 114–115

automaticity, 85, 139

beginners: asking for help by, 38–39; capable performers vs., 45; characteristics of, 28–29, 144; decision making by, 31–32, 69; description of, 27–28; failure to take responsibility for actions by, 33–36; lack of comfortable and efficient routines of, 36–37; learning by, 37–39; mentoring of, 38–39; planning skills of,

63; rational, procedural, and inflexible behavior of, 29–31; rules and established procedures for, 38, 40; summary of, 39

Bowden, Bobby, 16–17, 103

Branson, Richard, 19–20

Brooke, Alan, 62

Brown, Michael, 33–34

capable performers: action taking by, 52; beginners vs., 45; characteristics of, 43–44, 144; classification of problems by, 47; decision making by, 47–49, 51–54; experience of, 45; functional skills of, 44–45; learning resources developed by, 54–56, 58; leveraging of strengths by, 55; progression toward competence by, 56; responsiveness to situations by, 49–51, 57; rules and procedures used by, 50, 53; seeing similarities across contexts by, 46–47; skills of, 44–45; summary of, 56; focus on

capable performers, *cont'd*
  task requirements by, 44–45;
  timely decision making of, 47–49;
  use of strategic knowledge for
  decision making by, 51–54, 57
Casel, Alan, 106
change, 16
Chi, Michelene, 46
Churchill, Winston, 61–62
coaches, 73–74
colleagues, 54–55
Collins, Jim, 43–44
competency, 6
competent performers: abstract vs.
  concrete thought processes by, 66–
  67; action taking by, 61–64, 69–72;
  capable performers' progression
  toward, 56; characteristics of, 59–
  60, 144; coaches for, 73–74; critical
  skill development of, 78; decision
  making by, 61–64, 69–72; goal-
  oriented nature of, 61–64, 68–69;
  important factors distinguished
  from unimportant factors by, 64–
  67, 76; learning by, 73; long-term
  goal focus by, 63; mastery of rules
  by, 62; organization and, 60; planning by, 63, 67–69; progression to
  expert performer by, 73–74; reliability of, 73; summary of, 74
concrete thought processes, 66–67
contingency planning, 67–69, 77
Covey, Stephen, 64, 102
critical skills, 78
Cuban, Mark, 104–105

decision making: by beginners, 31–32,
  69; by capable performers, 47–49,
  51–54; by competent performers,
  61–64, 69–72; effects on coworkers, 72; by experts, 111–113; goals
  and long-term plans used in, 61–
  64, 75; intuitive, 111–113; momentum in, 69–72; organizational, 72;
  by proficient performers, 88–91,
  96; rules- and norms-based approach to, 31–32; situation-based
  approaches to, 50; strategic knowledge used in, 51–54, 57; timely, 47–
  49, 69–72
Donovan, Marion O'Brien, 64–65
Drucker, Peter, 13, 62

education, 135
Einstein, Albert, 50
empathetic listening, 102
Ericsson, Anders, 15–17, 137
established routines, 87–88, 95
experience(s): analyzing of, 15; applied skills learned from, 130–131;
  diversity of, 15; expanding of, 129;
  expertise development through,
  14–16; knowledge from, 18, 53,
  129; learning from, 37, 41, 131;
  making of, 128–130; performance
  not correlated with, 15–16; secondhand, 129–130; 24; strategic
  knowledge obtained from, 53;
  through networking, 133–135;
  uses of, 128
expertise: earliest works on stages of
  development of, 6; maintaining of,
  122–123; self-rating of, 8–10;
  summary of, 145
experts: action planning by, 126;
  action taking by, 19; attending to
  the atypical by, 107–109; automatic behavior by, 114–115; characteristics of, 99–100, 144; creation
  of, 11; definition of, 14, 99; executing of skills by, 113–115; failure as
  handled by, 116–120; goal setting
  by, 121; information gathering by,
  101–103; intuitive action by, 111–

113; keys to becoming, 13–14; knowledge of, 17–19; knowledge seeking by, 101–104; memory abilities of, 104–107; planning by, 109–113; proficient performers' progression to, 93–94; resources used by, 101; self-monitoring by, 120–122, 124; self-reflection by, 99–100; skills of, 100; summary of, 122–123; superior memory abilities of, 104–107; working to become, 11, 13

failure, 116–120
failure to take responsibility for actions, 33–36
Fasth, Niclas, 142–143
Feltovich, Paul, 17, 46
formal education, 135
forward thinking, 88–91
future events, predicting of, 91–92

Gates, Bill, 50, 135
general skills, 21–22
Glaser, Robert, 46
goals, 61–64, 121
Graham, Ann, 52

Hahn, Carl, 17
human interaction, 133–134
Humer, Franz, 111–113

important factors distinguished from unimportant factors, 64–67, 76
incompetency, 55
information gathering, 20, 85–86, 101–103
intelligence, 17–18
intuition, 111–113
Iverson, Ken, 80

Jobs, Steve, 135

Kelleher, Herb, 90–91
knowledge: alternatives and options developed through, 18; building of, 18; characteristics of, 17–19; clients as source of, 134; decision making based on, 51–54; from experience, 18, 129; experts' insatiable search for, 101–104; formal education for, 135; gaining of, 131–143; from human interaction, 133–134; importance of, 16–17, 131–132; limited, 29; organizing of, 132; from reading, 136–137; self-assessments, 25; sources of, 132–137; specialty-specific nature of, 17; strategic, for decision making, 51–54, 57; value of, 133–134; wisdom gained through, 133

LaBarre, Polly, 132
lack of control, 35
Lagasse, Emeril, 69
Land, Edwin, 46
learning: by beginners, 37–39; by capable performers, 54–56; by competent performers, 73; from competition, 73; from experience, 37, 41, 141; experience and, 14; by experts, 100–104; importance of, 16; mentoring for, 73; ongoing need for, 102; by proficient performers, 93–94, 97; of skills, 20, 138–139; trial-and-error, 37, 133
learning resources, 54–56, 58, 73, 94, 97
Lendl, Ivan, 86
leveraging of strengths, 55
Levi-Montalcini, Rita, 50–51
limited knowledge, 29
listening, empathetic, 102
Longfellow, Henry Wadsworth, 145
long-term plans, 61–64, 75

Mahadevan, Rajan, 104
Mann, Carol, 82
McCafferty, Michael, 70–71
McEnroe, John, 86
memory, 104–107
mentors: for beginners, 38–39, 42; description of, 20, 28; learning from, 73; meeting with, 42
Meyers, Aaron, 49
middle managers, 54–55
momentum, 69–72

networking, 125, 133–135
norms, 31–33

organization: decision making in, 72; rules and procedures of, 38, 40
outcomes, 72, 91

perceptual skills, 83–87
personal development, 6
personal responsibility, 80–83, 95
Pizzo, Vincent, 52
planning: by beginners, 63; by competent performers, 63, 67–69; contingency, 67–69, 77; by experts, 109–113; extensive level of, 109–111
practicing of skills, 137, 139–143
predicting of future events, 91–92
Prietula, Michael, 17
problems: solving of, 21
problem solving: capable performers' approach to, 47; experts' approach to, 100, 117–118; forward thinking used for, 88–91; proficient performers' approach to, 88–91
proficient performers: causes of problems identified by, 84; characteristics of, 79–80, 92–94, 144; decision making by, 88–91, 96; established routines used for everyday tasks by, 87–88, 95; forward thinking used for problem analysis and problem solving by, 88–91; learning by, 93–94, 97; perceptual skills of, 83–87; personal responsibility of, 80–83, 95; predicting of future events by, 91–92; problem solving by, 88–91; progression to expert by, 93–94; summary of, 94

reading, 136–137
responsibility: for actions, failing to take, 31–36; personal, 80–83, 95
responsiveness to situations, 49–51, 57
Roosevelt, Franklin, 61–62, 137
routines, 36–37, 87–88, 95
rules and procedures: beginners' use of, 31–33, 38, 40; breaking of, 50–51; capable performers' use of, 50, 53; competent performers' mastery of, 62; flexibility in following, 53

Sanborn, Mark, 81
Schultz, Howard, 136
secondhand experience, 129–130
selectivity, 67
self-monitoring, 120–122, 124
Semon, Waldo, 103
Shea, Fred, 81
similarities across contexts, 46–47
situational awareness, 84–85
situations: monitoring of, 108; outcomes based on reading of, 72, 91–92; responsiveness to, 49–51, 57
skills: anticipatory, 92; application of, 130–131; automaticity of, 85, 139; of beginners, 37; of capable performers, 44–45; critical, 78; development of, 19–22, 137–138; of experts, 20–22, 100, 113–115; general, 21–22; information-gathering, 20; learning of, 20, 138–139;

perceptual, 83–87; of proficient performers, 83–87; practicing of, 137, 139–143; selectivity, 67; self-assessments, 25; specific, 20
Smith, Dean, 109–110
Sorrell, Charlie, 105
strategic knowledge used in decision making, 51–54, 57

Tabuchi, Yoshihisa, 116
task requirements, 44–45
Taylor, William, 132
thought processes, 66–67
timely decision making, 47–49, 69–72

Traub, Marvin, 32
trial-and-error learning, 37, 133

Urban, Tom, 118–119

Walgreen, Charles, 108
Walton, Sam, 18–19, 47, 85–86, 122
Watson, Thomas J., Sr., 101
Welch, Jack, 72
Wooden, John, 2, 110
Wrigley, William Jr., 68

Yunus, Muhammad, 107–108